Opposite and above: **Children using their school grounds in break times for physical activities.**

With a little thought and imagination a wide range of activities can take place in the school grounds that will not only encourage pupils to enjoy lessons but will also provide them with a range of skills and ideas to try out in break and lunch times.

Every school is different, both in its grounds and in the needs of its pupils. However, all schools can make the most of what they have to increase the value of their PE curriculum. Many ideas in this book will be directly suitable for your school, while others will need adaptation, and some may not be appropriate at all. Difficulties may be overcome by changing the way you manage, use and develop your grounds. This might mean simple changes such as zoning areas for different types of play, encouraging pupils to act as arbitrators and referees, or providing smaller or larger equipment to widen the range of activities available. This could be anything from providing balls and hoops for pupils to play with, tracks and stages painted on the ground and walls, to adding basketball hoops and ball walls.

This book has been written for head teachers, subject leaders, class teachers and students looking for ideas for Physical Education in the grounds.

Chapter one offers suggestions for planning successful outdoor lessons. Advice is offered about the management and organisation of children and equipment. In Chapter two the health related aspects of teaching Physical Education are expanded and practical ideas are suggested for using the school grounds. The chapters following offer teachers a variety of activities to help them to meet the Programmes of Study for Physical Education using the school grounds. Chapter three gives ideas for athletic activities and organising sports days, Chapter four provides suggestions for a range of games, and Chapter five has a variety of stimulus ideas for dance. Chapter six offers gymnastic activities for the grounds and in Chapter seven ideas for outdoor and adventurous activities are explored. At the end of the book there are examples of worksheets for independent work by children and a list of References and Resources.

National Curriculum References

England and Wales
Physical Education
KS1 Health Related Exercise
KS2 Health Related Exercise
KS1 Programme of Study Games
KS2 Programme of Study Games
KS1 Programme of Study Gymnastic Activities
KS2 Programme of Study Gymnastic Activities
KS1 Programme of Study Dance
KS2 Programme of Study Dance
KS2 Athletic Activities
KS2 Outdoor and Adventurous Activities
English KS1 and KS2 Attainment Targets:
Speaking and Listening
Maths KS1 and KS2 Attainment Targets:
Number: Using and Applying Mathematics,
Shape, Space and Measures
Science KS1 and KS2 Attainment Targets:
Life Processes and Living Things
Design and Technology KS1 and KS2
Attainment Targets: Designing, Making
History KS1 and KS2
Geography KS1 and KS2
Art KS1 and KS2
Music KS1 and KS
Health Education

Scotland
Expressive Arts: Art and Design, Drama,
Music and Physical Education pp1–7
Attainment Outcomes:
Using materials, techniques, skills and media
Expressing feelings ideas, thoughts and
solutions
Evaluating and appreciating
Environmental Studies pp1–7 Science, Social
Subjects, Technology
Attainment Outcomes:
Understanding living things and the processes
of life
Understanding energy and forces
Understanding earth and space
Understanding people and place
Understanding people in the past
Understanding and using the design process

Health Education Attainment Outcomes :
Healthy and Safe Living:
Knowledge and Understanding ,
Taking Action on Health

Contents

Introduction

When people think about teaching in the school grounds, Physical Education (PE) is probably the first subject they think about. In many schools football and netball pitches dominate the grounds. Whilst it is important that there is enough space for teaching games, the grounds can be used much more imaginatively for all areas of the PE curriculum.

This book suggests ways in which many elements of PE, including gymnastics and dance, can be taught outside. Rarely do gymnastics or dance lessons use the outdoors as a stimulus or setting, but we often see children doing handstands and cartwheels outside in their free time. Similarly, for adventurous activities some schools think only in terms of using facilities away from the site, but many tasks and exercises can be carried out within the grounds, perhaps in preparation for a trip away.

Most children love going outside for PE. It is the highlight of the week. PE is especially enjoyable when the weather is fine and everyone is suitably dressed. Success and enjoyment in PE lessons will also encourage children to be active in their leisure time. Research evidence points to the fact that physical activity is good for us, and that people who have enjoyed physical activity as children go on to be active adults. It is hoped that the activities in this book will encourage a range of physical activities both within the school environment and beyond it.

Learning through Landscapes has highlighted the importance of the school grounds as 'a safe open space' for children, as their freedom to roam decreases. This space is especially important for physical activity. For some children the school grounds provide the only space in which they can feel free to run, chase and tumble; a place where they can climb, swing, turn upside-down and try out new skills.

Physical Education Outdoors

Be well prepared

For PE outdoors the lesson plan will be similar to the indoor lesson. Good planning is the key to a successful lesson. Preliminary preparation in the classroom will really help to make everything run smoothly. It is particularly important for the children to know what is expected of them before they leave the building. Diagrams of apparatus and plans or maps of the area can be discussed in the indoor space to make management and organisation in the outdoor space trouble free. It is also crucial that the parameters of the playing space are defined and that the children know the signal for coming back together. (A whistle is a very useful piece of apparatus!) Decide on all items of equipment before the lesson and be quite clear about who will carry it and where it can be most safely positioned.

INVOLVE THE CHILDREN

Children need to play some part in the process of planning and evaluating in Physical Education. It is an important element in being physically educated and is reflected in National Curriculum requirements. This might involve children being given some responsibility for selecting their own apparatus, making up their own warm ups, games or practices or finding creative ways of using the features of the grounds for physical activity. Generations of children have adapted and modified their own games to suit their surroundings and this ability can be used in PE lessons. A class project focused on using the grounds in creative ways could be put together using ICT skills. It could then be shared by other classes, thus building up a selection of activities that are special to your school.

Comfort

BE WARM

Children need to be appropriately dressed to enjoy their lessons, as do teachers. Too many people have developed negative attitudes towards physical activity because they remember being cold or uncomfortable on unsheltered playing fields. It is better when it is cold for everyone to wear a track suit or sweatshirt and to remove a layer when they have warmed up, than to wear just shorts and a T-shirt. Children lose a great deal of heat through their heads and a woolly hat will help to keep them warm and more comfortable on cold days. It is better for everyone to wrap up warmly and use the school grounds for games in winter than to use the weather as an excuse for always taking the lesson indoors.

Whenever the children go outside for PE, even in hot weather, a warm up is necessary for all the Programmes of Study.

Children at South Park I and J, Ilford, warmly dressed for PE outdoors.

BE COOL

In hot weather children should be encouraged to wear caps and use protective sun creams when playing outdoors, and they should be allowed to have a drink if necessary. Many activities can be played in shaded areas. The edge of a shadow under large bushes and trees can provide a defined playing area and boundary. This is where creative use of the space is important. When timetabling the use of the grounds a subject leader in PE needs to work out the sunny and shaded areas at different times of the year and day. Then s/he can try to provide a balance of opportunities for all the staff and pupils. Shaded areas are often more comfortable on hot days for children who need to observe the lesson or are waiting their turn at an activity.

At the end of all lessons a cooling down period will help the children to recover from vigorous activity, reflect on the main part of the lesson and prepare to return to the classroom in a controlled manner.

BE SAFE

Children need to know the rules for working outside to ensure that they and others are safe. The health and safety rules for swimming pools are always made very explicit in schools and yet rules for other areas of the PE curriculum are often less well defined. A whole school policy on safety and procedure needs to be discussed, agreed by all, and drawn up under the guidance of the subject leader.

Children are more likely to keep to rules if they understand the need for them and have also been consulted in the process. There needs to be careful inspection of the grass area if children are going to work at ground level in dance or gymnastic activities. The school policy also needs to address bare-foot work. Generally very light shoes are a better option than trainers for these activities.

The playground area should be dry and free from stones and other debris. Care needs to be taken to keep any playing area free from broken glass, holes and any stray equipment or obstacles.

The best guidance for all safety issues in PE is 'Safe Practice in Physical Education' BAALPE (1996), an essential document for all those involved in the organisation and implementation of Physical Education in primary schools.

Watching and listening in PE

The school grounds are always alive with interesting things for children to focus on and, naturally, they can be distracted by sounds and movement not directly related to the lesson of the day. It will help children to listen to instructions, share ideas and watch demonstrations if they are brought together so that all can see and hear. Ask the children to sit together and make sure they don't have the sun in their eyes. You might also think about the direction of the wind and the location of outdoor sounds when sharing ideas and giving instructions in the open air.

Children in a semi-circle listening to the teacher explaining an activity.

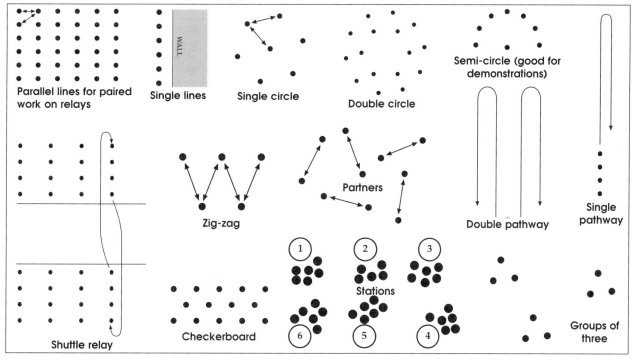

Organising children in small groups

Parallel lines for paired work on relays

Single lines

Single circle

Double circle

Semi-circle (good for demonstrations)

Zig-zag

Partners

Double pathway

Single pathway

Shuttle relay

Checkerboard

Stations

Groups of three

Organising children in open space

The organisation of games, relays or races on grass is much easier if there are grids, marked lines and boundaries.

When planning and teaching Games and Athletic Activities you might find the formations which are illustrated above very helpful. If there are markings on the surface to guide the children they will be able to take more responsibility for organising themselves into groups and teams.

ORGANISING EQUIPMENT

A lock-up store near the playground or field will make carrying easier for all concerned. To aid organisation there needs to be a variety of equipment with enough for every child: hooks and clips for sticks, bats and rackets; nets, buckets and crates for balls, quoits, discs and bean bags; and shelving with a lip to store large balls and athletic equipment. Large pieces of apparatus also need a designated space. Labelling will help all concerned to get the equipment in and out of the store quickly and safely. Colour coding will also make organisation and stocktaking easier. A few lightweight baskets in the corresponding colours can be used to enable the children to select equipment, carry it into the working space and take responsibility for looking after it. Children need to know that they must return all equipment after use. It doesn't take long for supplies to be depleted if each class loses even just one or two items.

USING WORKSHEETS FOR PE

Setting tasks for children in the grounds can be a challenge as the open space can make communication difficult. Preparation of worksheets for work outdoors will help with

Children carrying an equipment basket.

management and organisation. All PE is active so it is sometimes difficult for the children to hold the worksheets in their hands. Laminated cards held on a clip board will stop the worksheets from blowing away in the wind. Bean bags or pebbles are also good for weighing them down.

BOUNDARIES

Whether the boundaries are natural or imposed children need to know the extent of the general space in which they are moving. This can be explained before they leave the classroom. In the initial stages it is easier to manage a group in a more restricted space and then to extend the boundaries as the children's skills increase. Natural boundaries such as trees, bushes, hedges, walls or a slope can create limits in which activities should take place. Grids, lines and geometric shapes are excellent for organising the class and for enabling children to take some responsibility for planning and creating their own activities. Imaginative markings such as mazes, animal shapes, spaceships and stations, clocks, compasses, rivers, and games boards can stimulate inventive play in PE lessons and at playtime. Fences also provide natural boundaries though rules need to be established for when balls go over into neighbouring territory and out of play.

On the move

All aspects of the PE curriculum involve children moving in space. Whatever the playing area, shape or type of surface available, children need to be able to move together safely. The first visit to the playground or field can be exciting and even a bit overwhelming for very young children who may not be used to large open spaces. Even at Key Stage 2 some children have difficulty in moving with others in open space. For example, in tag games they run outside the lines to avoid being tagged. The reasons for this include lack of control in stopping or lack of understanding of the task or rules. In the beginning, even for the vigorous warm up, it is best to have children moving 'in place', ie running on their own mark or shape (see page 12), before expecting them to run freely in a controlled way in more open space.

Before any running or chasing activities are introduced ensure that the children are able move in a controlled manner in space without bumping into each other. Even very young children can understand that this is important for their own and others' safety if it is explained to them. Once they are able to walk, stop on a signal and jog at a slow pace then more complex tasks and activities may be enjoyed.

ON THE SPOT – INDIVIDUAL

Everyone in the class should be able to find and identify their own base for individual activities. Shapes either marked on the ground with chalk or rope, a hoop on grass or an individual mat with a shape will offer a 'home' for each child in movement activities. Children working in their own space can then concentrate on developing their proficiency without interference from others.

Children who have behavioural difficulties which result in them being disruptive in PE will find it easier to stay on task if they are given their own special place in the area in which to develop skills.

Once children are good at moving and responding in their own space they can practise and refine the skills of moving safely with others.

Traffic lanes allow several acitivities to take place simultaneously.

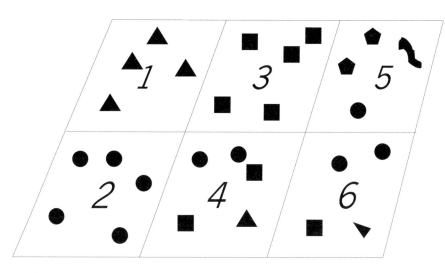

A grid marked with a variety of different shapes.

STOPPING WITH CONTROL

Teach the children to stop immediately on a signal. Some children find it quite difficult to stop from running fast and need to practise in open space. When running in the school grounds children should never be asked to run at a fence or a wall or to turn in relays or races. A slow-down area should always be included when estimating the length of any track. Lines marked on the ground are useful for this purpose.

> Remind children that they need to listen for any signal to stop and that stopping involves planting feet in a forward/backward stride position with flexion in the ankle, knee and hip to absorb force. Heads should be up with eyes looking forward, arms slightly out to the side to balance the body. The body weight is brought back and down over the base of support to gain control.

Infants need to experiment with different ways of ' finding their feet ' in this new environment and activities could include:

- Walking in the general space using as much space as possible, avoiding others by changing direction, walking forwards, backwards, sideways and along different pathways on the playground.
- Using imaginary pathways, eg wiggly or zig-zag, to spell out own names or names of heroes or pop stars. Vary the speed and the force of the walking, ie quickly, slowly, heavily or lightly. Develop this by making simple patterns.

- Extending the idea to children working in pairs, leading and following, away from and back to base, getting faster in their movements. This might involve:
- Travelling on feet in a variety of ways, ie walking, hopping, skipping, galloping or jogging within boundaries. When children arrive at a line, rope, slope or marker, balance along the boundary or travel along it in a different way.

This could be extended in group activities.

Moving together

Squirrels in the trees
Equipment: Individual place markings or individual mats.
Any number of children.
This is suitable for young children. In this game children have their own base and on the direction from the teacher move away from the base with, for example, springy jumps. On the signal 'Squirrels back to trees' they race back to their special place as quickly as possible.

Find and follow a leader
Equipment: bands for half the number in the group.
Any number of children.
Half the children in the class wear bands and will be leaders. The other children will be followers. All children jog freely together in all directions on grass or on tarmac. On a signal followers trail the leader next to them and follow the direction of their pathway. If the grounds have mounds, trees or bushes the routes will be more exciting. After 30 seconds change to all jogging freely again. Repeat and change the roles frequently.

During this simple activity check that the children are using all the available space and remind them not to bunch together. It is quite difficult to follow a leader and avoid others at the same so it takes lots of practice.

Health Related Exercise

Positive attitudes and safe practices

Throughout Key Stages 1 and 2 children should be helped to develop positive attitudes to physical activity and health, and learn safe practices. Every opportunity should be taken to help children to have a better understanding of how the body works, to know how to take part in physical activity safely and discover activities which they enjoy. This will help them to develop positive attitudes towards healthy physical activity.

The school grounds can provide opportunities for children to experiment with their own games and to test their strength and wits against themselves and others. They can make up running and chasing games for warm ups, and experience other activities which are specifically beneficial in developing cardiovascular health, flexibility, muscular strength and endurance. There are several suggestions in this section.

Warming up

Even on hot days children need to warm up. The body needs to be properly prepared for all forms of physical activity and, from an early age, children can begin to understand why this is important. Many of the concepts explored in Science and Health Education can be reinforced in Physical Education.

Warming up will involve gradually raising the pulse rate with some gentle jogging activities and then, when the muscles are warm, stretching the muscles and mobilising the joints. Once the muscles and joints are loosened up more vigorous, fun running games can be played. These games, which involve running and chasing, and changing direction, are best played on open ground, as long as boundaries have been established. Examples of these games, eg. *Tag tails*, *The Smelly, Welly, Nelly, Jelly game*, and *Caterpillar tag* can be found in Bray (1993). If the grounds are spacious, children can run freely, chase each other, learn how to control their bodies, change direction and pace and learn the principles of warming up safely.

Fill the Space (whole body stretch)
As a group children all stretch as widely as possible to fill up as much space as they can by touching other children's finger tips and toes!

Below left: Children warming up – running, chasing, changing direction, etc. open ground.
Below right: Children running 'in place' on individual mats.

Remember:

Muscles should be stretched slowly, bouncing or jerking movements should be avoided. Remind children how cats stretch their bodies. Hold the stretch for a few seconds and repeat. The warm-up exercises should be appropriate to the activities which are to follow, for example if the activity is throwing, shoulders, arms and legs need to be well warmed up. Gently does it!

Going nowhere! (to stretch the leg muscles)
Lift one leg high with knees bent, similar to a marching action with pointed toes. Hold at the highest point for a count of four. Repeat with the other leg.

Ankle circles (to mobilise the ankles)
Stand on the left foot with the toes of the right foot on the ground near the left foot. Carefully circle the right ankle four times, then repeat with the left ankle. Look around for circular shapes in the environment. Select one: is it big or small? Draw it with your toes. Look at different shapes around you, for example leaf shapes. Choose one and draw it with your feet.

Shoulder circles (to mobilise the shoulders)
Feet shoulder-width apart, arms hang down, circle both shoulders by rounding them forwards, towards a landmark in the grounds, lift them up and back and gently bring them down.

Shoulder stretch (to stretch the shoulder muscles)
Stand with feet shoulder-width apart and knees slightly bent. Hold both hands together and lift arms above the head to the sky. Pull in tummy and feel the stretch around the shoulders.

Reach for the limits (to stretch the sides of the body)
Stand with feet shoulder-width apart. Stretch right arm above the head with fingers reaching outwards towards the limits of the area. Lower to hip height and repeat with the left arm.

Hip circles (to mobilise the lower back)
Stand with feet shoulder-width apart, knees slightly bent, arms relaxed by sides. Circle the hips to the right, backwards, to the left and forwards using the tummy muscles.

GO FOR IT!

Here are some ideas for vigorous warm up games:
Touch wood, metal, stone or plastic
Children run freely in the space and, on a signal, run to find and touch wood, metal, stone or plastic, as called by the teacher.

North, south, east and west
Children run freely in the space and, on a signal either run to north, south, east or west in the area. If compass designs are available on the playground this idea could be extended to children running freely and, on the signal, forming lines, circles or other shapes at the various compass points.

These two girls are using school equipment for stretching exercise.

Frost and Sun
Three children are nominated as the catchers (Frosts) and three children as the releasers (Suns). All children run in the space and when caught by the Frosts freeze in position or do star jumps on the spot until released by the Suns.

Shadow touch (a game for a sunny day)
Children play in pairs and attempt to step on a partner's shadow. When they do, they call 'Gotcha' and change roles.

Bee's knees (a good game for an uneven number of children)
One child is the leader (the Bee's knees), other children each have a partner and jog about in the space, side by side. The Bee's knees calls out different body parts, eg back to back, four hands together in the air, four feet together in the air (on dry days!) etc and the children stop and respond. On the call 'Busy Bee' all children including the leader rush to find a different partner. A new leader emerges as the Bee's knees. Once children are used to the game it is best played at a fast pace.

The creature game
Children run freely in the space and the teacher calls out the names of various insects or animals. Children move at the speeds and directions suggested by the particular creature, eg spider fast and slow, forwards, backwards and sideways; wasp fast and direct, high and low; slug slow and meandering; mouse fast and free; rabbit fast and bouncing in different directions. Other ideas involve children

getting together in small groups on the signal (this can cause a lot of giggles!). For example, on the word ladybird, children get together in threes and move their six legs together; on spider they get together in fours and move their eight legs together; on centipede they get together as a whole group and attempt to coordinate leg movements.

Rainbow tag
Equipment: coloured mats, or coloured shapes painted on the playground. An equal number of each colour are needed for this game. Coloured braids.
Children are divided into colour groups of equal size and wear a braid of the corresponding colour. They could be grouped by ability for this game.

The equipment is spaced out about the area and there is one less item than the number of children in each group. One child in each group is the catcher who may only tag children in his/her own colour. Children run from one mat or shape to the other of their own colour (these are safe havens) trying to avoid being tagged. Any child tagged changes places with the catcher.

Change the catcher regularly if necessary.

Cooling down
It is important that children experience a gradual decrease in physical activity to recover after vigorous exercise. Some stretching will help to prevent muscle soreness. A calming activity can help children to return to the classroom ready to focus on the next activity.

Left and above opposite:
Fitness trails are fun and help children practise different skills.

Go for a gentle jog along the lines on the field or playground.

Put on track suit tops and any clothing removed during the warm up and gently stretch out the main muscles used.

Developing fitness: a fitness trail in your school

A fitness trail can be fun and challenging. It can be used during PE lessons, freely at play times or as part of joint community use. Natural features in the grounds are ideal for setting the scene and often very little equipment is needed to create colourful, stimulating routes around the grounds. Children can select their own pathways and either challenge themselves to go further or increase the demands of the exercise as they get fitter. They can take some responsibility for recording and evaluating their own performance. Concepts learned in health/body projects may be reinforced along the way.

The children will experience a well-balanced fitness programme if the station activities focus on specific body parts, for example: Station 1, legs; Station 2, arms; Station 3, stomach; Station 4, legs/trunk strengthening activities.

USE NATURAL FEATURES

Logs, trees, slopes, dips and hollows, tunnels and walls can all be used for activities, as can ropes, climbing equipment, netting, benches and mats. Markings on the playground or field can be adapted in a variety of ways. For example, they can be used to run around or for going to and fro. They might be used for jumping activities or as targets for throwing. (Wendy Collin has offered some sound advice to Devon teachers and many of her ideas are suggested here.)

THE ROUTE

Organise stations 150-200 metres apart and make interesting routes around the space available. When planning the route it is important to take account of all the children, including those with special educational needs. Ensure that routes are suitable for children in wheelchairs. Colour coding can help in the organisation, for example the green route is easier and requires six repetitions of the exercises, the red route requires eight repetitions and the black route ten repetitions.

Children will also have good ideas of their own to add to the plan and these should be encouraged. A science, health or technology project can be incorporated in a group-work exercise planning a fitness trail. Children can devise their own activities, draw up the plans and make the station instructions for all to enjoy. The instructions should be :

worded clearly and simply to be understood easily;

sketched if necessary to be accessible to all.

As the routes need to be easily seen outdoors:

laminate instruction cards or paint instructions on hard wood and fix to wooden stakes, fences, goal posts or walls;

mark arrows on cards or the surface to point to the next station.

Don't forget to cater for differing levels of physical fitness, size and ability.

Using the trails

Ask children to look at the whole trail and see where it goes. Suggest that they choose the colour route which they feel suits their fitness and ability.

Remind them of the importance of a warm up before starting. They should begin with gentle jogging, then some stretching exercises for a few minutes. Initially this will be teacher led but, as children get more used to using the trails, they can warm up independently

Tell them that they may begin at any station, but it is best to choose one where there are few other children.

Stress the importance of doing the exercises properly. A demonstration by yourself or another child might help.

CHALLENGES

See if they can get around all the stations. Then ask the children to work in pairs and tell each other how they might improve the way they do the exercises.

Set time challenges for individual or team events, eg How fast? Can you beat your last performance?

Ask children to repeat the same colour route several times, and then suggest that they might like to move up to the next colour.

STATIONS

Wall sit

Ask children to 'sit' with their backs flat against a wall imagining that they are sitting on a chair. Hold for five seconds and repeat. This is good for strengthening the legs.

Wall press-ups

Children need to face a wall and keeping their feet away from it. Lean forward and put hands flat on the wall about level with shoulders with arms straight and fingers pointing upwards. Feet must be firmly planted on the ground. The body should be straight and at an angle. Their arms need to bend to take the top part of the body close to the wall. Remind the children to take care not to bump their noses on the wall! From this position they push away, and then repeat the exercise.

Pull-ups on a bar

Children begin by hanging from a bar with two hands, feet off the ground.

Pull up until the chin is level with the bar and then gently return to the starting position.

This task could be performed three times, with a short rest and then repeated.

Bunny jumps

These can be done over a fixed log, a series of tyres, into and out of large tyres, hoops or circles or either side of a straight line.

Bunny jumps

Wall press-ups

Pull-ups on a bar

Safe sit-ups

Feet off the ground on a rope

On top of the world
Ask children to run up a slope, turn and run down. A marker to separate the up route from the down route will help children to avoid each other when they are running down the slope. This is repeated until they get to the top for the fifth time where they do five star jumps. If they have the energy this can be repeated.

Balancing tricks
Ask children to leap over 'stepping stones' or balance along logs without falling over. Increasing the speed will increase the challenge.

Climbing ropes, frames or across bridges
Ask children to:
hang on to a rope with two hands and with feet off the ground stay for half a minute.

Swing on the ropes
If double ropes are available, use two ropes to turn a somersault.
Repeat.
For other ideas along these lines see Bray (1993), Harris and Elbourn (1997).

Parachute games

The open space, and perhaps a gentle breeze, with the sky as a back cloth, make parachute games ideal for the school grounds. These games will also help children to:
develop upper body strength, especially in the shoulders, arms wrists and fingers;
cooperate;
develop listening skills;
further develop their basic movement skills.
Parachutes vary in size but approximately 12 children can enjoy these activities.

STRETCHES
Spread the parachute flat on the ground. Begin with everyone sitting around the edge and facing the centre. Children are asked to hold the edge and pull back away from the centre. Take it easy at first and gently stretch the muscles. This may also be tried from kneeling or standing positions.

Moving under the mushroom
Begin with children kneeling on one knee and raising and lowering the 'chute to create a mushroom effect. Progress to children standing and raising their arms high and then crouching down to the ground to create a more dramatic effect. The children take it in turns to move across the space under the raised 'chute in different ways, for example like mini beasts: spiders crawl; flies rush swooping high and low; grasshoppers hop; butterflies flutter; slugs and snails cross slowly; moths dart quickly.

This could link with a science activity after children have watched the movements of creatures in the grounds.

Fluffy clouds
Children cooperate by beginning to move the parachute gently and then aim to create a ripple effect by moving hands up and down, increasing the intensity to a billowing effect.

Sounds in the grounds
Ask children to sit on the ground around the parachute and listen to the sounds around them. They may hear traffic, shouts, sirens, animals, horns, silence. Use the sounds as a stimulus to vary the speed and create the moving rhythm of the parachute.

Chase around the parachute
Children are spaced evenly around the parachute and each is given a name of a tree, flower or creature. Ask the children to stretch out the parachute and raise it like an umbrella. As it reaches its highest level the teacher calls out a name and all children who were given that name run clockwise around the circle and try to tag the person in front of them, before they get back to place.

Another version of this is to give children numbers or names. When their number or name is called they exchange places across the space underneath the 'chute with another who has the same number or name.

Hail stones
Children are spaced evenly around the parachute. Ten small, soft foam balls are placed on the parachute. Children shake the parachute to try to make them jump up and down like hail stones falling on a playground. How high can they make the balls jump?

Race the dandelion clocks
(12 children at a time can play this game and take turns to make it a timed competition.)

Children are each given a number from 1 to 12 and 12 beanbags are placed in the centre, under the parachute. On a signal, the parachute is raised to its highest level and number 1 starts by running underneath to collect one beanbag. S/he takes it back to place followed by number 2, etc. The challenge is: How quickly can the team collect all the beanbags whilst another child 'times' them by blowing out dandelion clocks?

Colour exchange (a game for a multicoloured parachute)
Children space out around the parachute and hold a particular coloured section. They inflate the parachute and, when a feature of the grounds is called, children stationed at the corresponding colour run underneath to change places with a child who was holding a section of the same colour. For example 'grass' children on the green section change, 'buttercup' children on the yellow section change, 'bricks' children swap over on the red section.

Rollaball
A large ball is placed on the parachute and children cooperate to roll it around the outside of the parachute and toss it high in the air to catch it. Once they have the control to move the

Race the dandelion clock!

ball together, the challenges can be increased. On a signal, the ball has to be manoeuvred towards the direction of named features in the grounds, eg towards the pond, from the fence to the school gate, close to the grass, high in the sky.

Simon says
The familiar game which is often played in primary schools can be extended using a parachute. The instruction from the teacher can relate directly to the grounds, eg 'parachute on the grass', 'parachute to the sky', 'move like a strong wind/gentle breeze', 'look at the surroundings ... be sharp! be smooth! be jagged! be undulating!' 'sit down', 'stand up! turn around!'

Inside out
Children space out around the parachute and raise and lower it on a signal. When the parachute is at its maximum height, all turn around to face outwards and then lie down facing upwards, to pull the chute downward and around their necks with heads inside and bodies sticking out. Guaranteed to raise a few giggles!

Creepy creature
The above idea can be extended with the children all stepping their legs in a clockwise direction to make the whole 'creature' move around. Ideas can be developed from creatures seen in the grounds. This can also be tried in a different way with children ending up lying with heads outside the chute and bodies underneath.

Golf match
Children are divided into two teams on opposite sides of the parachute and each have four small balls. The balls are of two different colours. By lifting and lowering the parachute each team tries to 'pot ' all their own coloured balls down the hole in the middle. If any balls fall off the side they do not count and have to be replaced on the chute. If all the green balls are potted first, the green team wins that round.

Creating games
Ask children to work in small groups and make up simple games using features in the grounds as targets. Examples of targets are tunnels, markings on the ground, walls or fences, posts, trees, skittles positioned on

mounds. The task might be 'select one or two items of equipment to send to the target (bean-bags, quoits, balls of various sizes, hoops, discs, frisbees). The game must involve every-one being busy and active and it must be a challenging one. If you are successful at hitting the target regularly, try to make the game more challenging for you. How can you do this?' (Select a smaller target in the grounds, or move further away.) (See worksheet on Page 51)

Relaxing

A quiet place to let children take time out and relax can be set aside in the school grounds. This could be a perfumed garden, a small grassed area, or a butterfly garden as created at Derwendeg Primary School.

In this special place children can be alone with their own thoughts. The open space can be utilised on a fine day to teach children how to relax; this can be part of a lesson. If the grass is dry ask children to lie down on their backs and close their eyes. They could bring their track suit tops or jumpers outside to use for a pillow if that is more comfortable.

A few moments spent encouraging children to recognise muscle tension and how to release it will help them to cope well when faced with stressful situations.

It is impossible to be agitated and relaxed at the same time, so learning to relax can have a calming effect. To help children recognise the difference between tense and relaxed muscles try contrasting how they might feel:

as hard as stone and then as soft as moss;

as hard as iron, then as soft as fluffy clouds.

Suggest that they try to tell their muscles to relax to make their bodies feel heavy and warm all over. Ask them to listen for sounds: birds, insects, bushes and trees rustling in the breeze, traffic, or people talking nearby. See if they can isolate and focus on one sound.

Other thoughts which may help them to concentrate and calm down include:

funny things;

special holidays;

kind things they would like to do for other people;

nice things other people have done for them;

favourite pets;

best friends.

Recharge batteries

Encourage children to take time out during playtime and even during curriculum time. An opportunity to relax for a while will be welcomed by children of all ages. Very rarely are they given time and space for that very special moment. There could be no better place than the school grounds. On a lovely day, encourage them to have some space, listen to the sounds, feel the warmth of the sun and have a little time for themselves.

Suggest you all find a quiet place in the grounds, close your eyes, feel comfortable and take the time to feel calm and just think about all the nice things that make you happy and smile. Try to imagine them and see them in your mind.

The Butterfly playground at Derwendeg PS in Glamorgan has been based on the life cycle of a butterfly.To the left is the 'chrysalis' growing willow tunnel, perfect for hide and seek. The smallest logs are yellow 'eggs' on the outline of an oak leaf which is a good place to practise balancing.

The Krypton Challenge health and fitness day at Derwendeg PS, Glamorgan. Mothers, fathers and even grandparents competed with the children at the many stations of activity (see page 21).

Health and fitness: celebration days

Some schools hold special activity days or have a whole week devoted to health issues. These may include a range of sports and physical challenges to provide opportunities for children to enjoy familiar activities and try out new ones.
Derwendeg Primary School in Wales enjoyed a Krypton Challenge in their school grounds. This involved parents and children and a sports personality who was well known in the community. In this event children were sponsored for each lap by friends and family to raise funds. However schools might also consider similar activities just for the fun of taking part.

ORGANISATION

There were 10 stations of activity and 10 parents volunteered to supervise a station each. All children in the school took part. Within two hours 360 children had completed the challenge. Children worked together with 6 children in each team. Each team consisted of mixed age ranges with infants and juniors working together and two classes completed the course in parallel.

The activities were clearly displayed on boards at each station and included Rugby Relay, Knock 'em Down, Score Goals, Shuttle Run/Walk, Shooting, Balance Beam, Hop into Square, Skipping/Jog on the Spot, Bouncy Castle, Climb Frame.

Valley School Kirkcaldy, Fife Regional Council, Scotland also enjoyed a Health and Fitness Day.
The day was divided into two events. The whole school took part – Nursery to Primary 7 (approximately 330 pupils).

ORGANISATION

Start 9.15am. Stewards, Teachers, School staff, parents and child care students supervised the activities. Each activity lasted approximately 15 minutes.
Flexible break time between 10.00am and 11.00am. During this time: nursery/lower primary children joined activities, staff had coffee/tea, children collected snack/tuck and milk and had a sit-down break under trees. Up to 15 minutes allowed for break. Rejoined activities at appropriate station.

Morning Activities
10 'stations' were located throughout the extensive playing fields and two hard surface playgrounds.
 1. Tag games suited to each age group.
 2. Selected activities.
 3. Victorian playground games. Back in time with 'stern Miss Brice' and the daily drill routine.
 4. Parachute games supervised by the visiting PE Specialist.
 5. Traditional Skipping and Ball Games.
 6. Team games suited to each age group.
 7. Games to encourage fine motor skills.
 8. Pop-lacrosse.
 9. Circuit practice for Mini Marathon.
10. Beat the goalie.

Afternoon Activity: mini marathon
Children gave completed lap cards to teachers who stapled the card to a sponsor form as evidence of successful completion.

Above: **Krypton Challenge: copy of boards displaying activities, plus certificate.**
Below: **Location map and activity programme from mini marathon at Kirkcaldy School.**

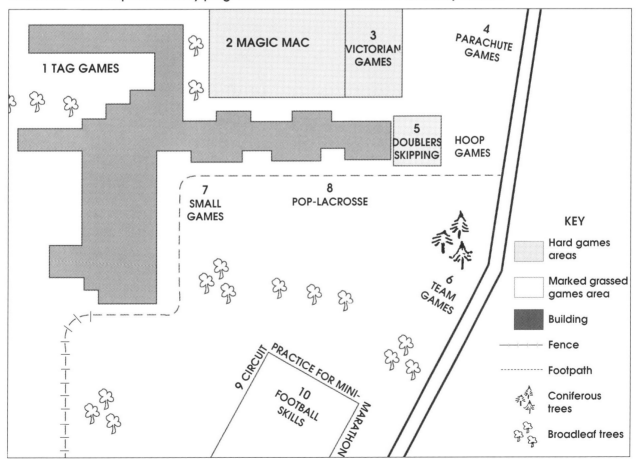

Nutrition

At Key Stages 1 and 2 children need to know that exercise uses energy which comes from food and drink. They also should be helped to understand that if the energy intake is greater than energy expenditure the body stores the excess as fat.

In some grounds children have the opportunity to grow fruit, vegetables or herbs. This might be in beds, tubs, grow bags or pots. This will give children opportunities to experiment with different soils, learn about planting and different feeding regimes. It will also enable children to learn about the food values and appreciate the nourishment which they may get from fresh produce. Lessons about nutrition can be reinforced in a fun way through games and activities, linking well with Science and Health Education. This might involve warm-up games where children have to identify the vitamins or minerals in named foods and fulfil tasks to demonstrate that they know the answers. For example:

What's in it for us?

Markings on the playground or field, coloured hoops or shapes made from small cones or markers are designated the areas for different vitamins or minerals. Children jog about the areas. The teacher calls out names of different vegetables and children identify the main vitamin or mineral source and run to stand in the right area as quickly as possible. For example, if vitamins are the focus of the activity and 'carrots' or 'spinach' are called they run to the area designated to vitamin A, 'tomatoes' or 'blackcurrants' to the vitamin C area, 'peas' or 'cabbage' to the area for vitamin B.

Calories – burn them up!

Children jog about the area and the teacher calls out different foods or combinations of foods. If they recognise that the food has a high sugar content the children run fast on the spot and shout 'Burn it up!' For example, call out 'sweets' and 'fizzy drinks' which contain lots of sugar. A similar game could be played using high fat content foods, for example, 'sausage and chips', 'beefburgers and chips'. When they recognise a food as having high fat content they shout 'Run it off!' and run fast on the spot.

Playtime games are fun.

Keep the colds away – Atishoo!

Children are given a group name, eg Sneeze, Wheeze, Sniff or Snuffle. The teacher then tells the story below while they listen for their word. For example, if they are in the group named Sneeze and they hear sneeze mentioned they run from one end of the space to the other, as do other groups when they hear their group name mentioned. When Atishoo (or a tissue) is heard, all children, regardless of which side of the space they are on, run to the other side of the space.

The story:

During the winter months many children suffer from colds and 'flu and they Sneeze, and they Wheeze, and they Sniff and they Snuffle in which case they often need a tissue. Fruits with lots of vitamin C like oranges and blackcurrants can help them when they Sneeze and they Wheeze and go Atishoo and Sniff and Snuffle. Eating lots of greens, tangerines and mandarins which contain vitamin C can help to prevent them going Atishoo or needing to Sneeze and Wheeze and Sniff and Snuffle. If they ate more fresh fruit and veg it might stop them from going Atishoo! Atishoo! (pause) ... Atishoo!

How the body works

A giant body painted on the playground can form the basis for amusing and worthwhile activities to help children recognise the short-term effects of exercise on the body. This has been found to be an excellent way of combining Science and Physical Education lessons. Simple concepts such as: muscles need energy to work and energy is used up during exercise; our bodies get food from eating and drinking and oxygen from breathing; energy gets to the muscles through the blood; when lots of energy is used up the blood gets low in oxygen; the lungs provide more oxygen through breathing; the heart pumps oxygenated blood out to the muscles; may be reinforced through playing games in the outdoor space.

Draw a body with heart and lungs (in blue indicating less oxygen and red indicating more oxygen). Instructions marked on the diagram, eg arrows indicate the flow of the circulatory system.

Children jog on the spot and do exercises at the muscles section, then visit the chambers of the heart and collect blue ribbons (top – in, bottom – out), arrive at the left side of the lungs and, wearing blue ribbons begin to exercise. Breathing in through mouth and nose pass through lungs, throw off blue ribbons and collect red ribbons. Continue on to the red in-chamber and out the out-chamber of the heart back to the muscles of the limbs.

The children then go on a jogging journey, travelling the pathway of the circulatory system.

For more ideas along these lines see Bray 1993, and Harris and Elbourn, 1997.

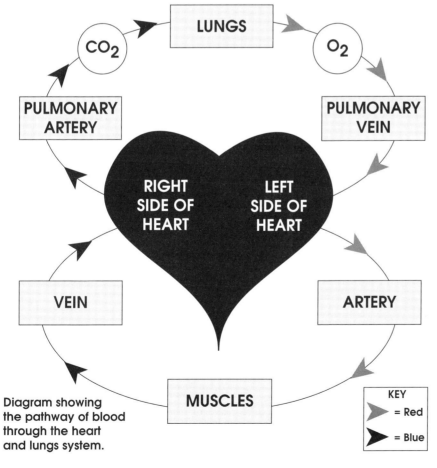

Diagram showing the pathway of blood through the heart and lungs system.

KEY
= Red
= Blue

Body drawn on the playground.

Athletic Activities

Organising activities

Athletic activities are best organised outdoors. Even if space is limited small groups of children can be set challenges to run more efficiently, to jump higher or further and to improve their skills of throwing. Self improvement is the essence of the programme. At this stage of their development it is important that they feel good about themselves and recognise that, with practice, they are all capable of success in improving their own performance. If too much emphasis is placed on competition between children in the class all but the naturally gifted will fail to experience a sense of achievement in this programme of study. For this reason small group activities set up in different areas will really help you to design tasks to match your learners' needs. Don't forget, all children are capable of improving their own performance; they just need plenty of encouragement, good teaching and lots of opportunities to practise their skills.

Use existing playground or field markings to set throwing and jumping challenges and look to the open spaces for running and distance events. If you use the IBM Ten Step Award you will find it helpful to have the markings which are suggested for implementation of the scheme permanently marked on the playground or field.

Sports day uses skills and style.

Running

During the warm up for athletic activities children can experiment with different ways of running.

ALONE AND IN A GROUP

On the spot on markings on playground or field, eg spots, circles, squares.

In grids – running forwards, backwards, to the left, to the right, running diagonally.

Around circles of any size running clockwise or anti-clockwise to change direction, once, twice, three times.

On marked lines (keep to the pathways), straight, wiggly, zig-zag, with sharp turns and changes of direction.

Around obstacles or shapes on the ground, for example, squares, circles, triangles, stars.

Over ropes or hurdles both single or marked on various surfaces.

With different stride patterns, eg long steps, high knees over parallel lines.

Pace running in a defined area with a partner, in a small group or as a class.

To help children to develop a good style of running, remind them that they need to:
Keep heads up when running;
Lean into the run slightly and lift knees;
Swing their arms which should be bent at the elbow freely (the leg speed will be influenced by the arm speed);
Put heels down first and push off from the balls of their feet;
Run lightly.

GROUP ACTIVITIES

Journey around the grounds

Children are in small groups (four or six) and jog about the space in single file. On a signal, the last person in each line jogs to the front to take the lead on a journey around the grounds. They can decide which places to visit. Jogging continues until all in the group have had an opportunity to take the lead.

Run around the country or the world!
A course is set up around the playground or field and children run it at their own pace and plot their progress as individuals, class or group on a chart in the classroom.

For example, each marker in the grounds represents 100 miles. Count the miles accumulated individually as a group or class and plot progress on a map. The distances could be related to actual places, eg 100 miles from the school to London.

The dressing up race.

Shooting stars
Children jog in single file or around the circumference of a circle, square or rectangle and on the signal, 'Shooting Stars!' sprint away from the area with a short burst of activity and then jog back to repeat.

Race tracks
If tracks are marked on the playground or field children will enjoy making up small group games using them as a stimulus.

For example, the teacher calls out types of cars and children respond with different ways of moving, eg Rolls Royce – smooth and stately; learner driver – stop, stutter and go; sports car – fast; old crock – three steps forward and one step back. The tracks can also be used to practise games skills on the move, for example: children dribbling a ball by bouncing basketball style; with a stick to practise hockey skills or with feet to master control for football. The pathways can be varied, eg the ball goes straight

and feet go on a zig-zag route, or the ball is dribbled on the track and feet run outside the lines for hockey and basketball skills.

Traffic lights
Tracks can form good boundaries for children to run along for traffic light games where the teacher calls out the colours of traffic lights and children respond. Green – all go running fast; amber – running on the spot, and red – all stop!

Jumping
How high?
Children can evaluate their efforts for height in jumping by marking the extent of the jump against an outside wall. A large ruler marked on a wall can be used for a variety of activities, eg measuring the height of jumps or children's growth. Alternatively, if no ruler is marked, ask them to use a piece of chalk and stand sideways to the wall with feet flat on the

Jumping high and making shapes in the air.

ground. Reach up as far as possible to make a mark. Next, jump and stretch up as high as possible to make a second mark on the wall at the highest point of the vertical jump. Tell them that the distance between the two marks is the distance recorded.

> To help children to gain maximum height in the jump and to land safely remind them to:
>   bend knees and ankles on take off and landing;
>   use a two-footed take off and landing;
>   'explode' quickly and forcefully, looking upwards, swinging arms upwards to stretch and reach with the arm nearest to the wall.

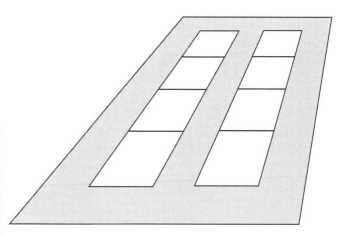

Diagram showing layout of mats for jumping.

How far?

Gymnastic mats taken outside onto the grass will provide a surface for jumping activities. Putting several mats together longways will provide a good expanse of surface to enable children to work in small groups for their jumping activities.

> To help children to develop their jumping technique remind them to:
>   bend their knees;
>   take arms back and then swing them forcefully forward, exploding from the crouched position by pushing off with toes leaving the ground last;
>   stretch and reach forwards;
>   bring knees into chest in preparation for landing;
>   heels touch the ground first on landing;
>   allow the knees and ankles to give on landing;
>   fall forwards;
>   arms and legs need to be coordinated in the jumping action.

CHALLENGES

Beat your record

Begin with both heels on the edge of the mat and jump as far as possible. Mark the distance covered from the edge of the mat to the back of heels on landing. Have six more tries to see if the distance can be bettered. Only move the mark if the distance is greater on subsequent attempts. Record the longest jump.

How far together?

Children work with a partner of similar ability. The first child jumps and makes a mark; the second tries to jump to the exact spot to match the distance. Change the leader and total scores of successful jumps .

Add it up

Groups of four children have several attempts at jumping their furthest distance along the mats. The best of each individual attempt is recorded and the four scores are then totalled to give a team score. This activity could be made more competitive by comparing the scores with other teams.

Another way of presenting this idea is to have teams competing to see which group can travel furthest along the mats with standing jumps. Children have several attempts to develop their skills before the scores are recorded. The first person in the team jumps and a line is drawn across the mat with chalk, a bean bag or rope placed at the point of landing; this is the starting line for the second member of the team and so on. A marker is then placed at the finishing point.

These activities are good for teams of mixed ability with all concerned contributing to the total score.

Throwing

How far?

Large open spaces in the school grounds provide wonderful opportunities for children to develop their long-distance throwing skills. It is quite possible that this will be the only place most children will have to throw high and far in open space. A system of rules for safe practice in throwing activities needs to be established in every school.

A good variety of bean bags, balls of different weights and sizes, wellies, foam javelins and discus will give children chances to practise and refine these skills. Throwing bean bags against a high wall can provide good practice for throwing for distance. The action of throwing hard and aiming high is what is needed to throw long distances.

> To help children to develop their skills of overarm throwing for distance remind them to:
> grip the object with the fingers;
> turn sideways with weight on the back foot;
> take the throwing arm back in preparation;
> point the opposite arm in the direction of the throw, aim high to throw far;
> the elbow leads as the arm moves forward;
> step forward on the opposite foot;
> release the object as the arm extends.

CHALLENGES

Throw the object as far as possible. Put a bean bag on the spot where it lands. Try to beat the distance with the next throw.

In pairs or in small groups take turns to throw. Measure the distance of each throw and add the best together.

Practice is needed to throw a ball properly.

Scores can be kept each lesson, the challenge being to improve the distance, or compared with other pairs or groups on a competitive basis week by week.

How many?
Hitting targets is great fun, especially when children feel that they are getting better all the time at increasingly difficult tasks. Funny faces painted on walls provide good targets against which children can test their accuracy in throwing. A bullseye nose offering a high score can add extra motivation for accurate throwing.

Dart boards, hearts, diamonds, triangles, circles and squares permanently painted or drawn in chalk by children will provide challenging targets and motivation for improvement in accurate throwing.

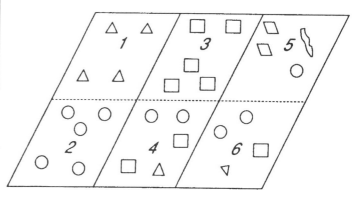

Interesting targets for a games area (taken from Games Activities in the Primary School, Hertfordshire CC).

> Equipment for underarm throwing at targets: (small balls, beanbags)
> To help children to be successful in throwing underarm at targets remind them to:
> look at the target;
> step forward on the opposite foot as the throwing arm swings backwards;
> have knees slightly bent;
> keep fingers facing the target as the throwing arm swings forward;
> release the object at about waist height;
> use the opposite arm to balance the body.

A ball in the bucket race on Sports day.

Add it up!
Children throw the object to land on the numbers on snake shapes, clock faces or over lines marked with numbers and try to accumulate high scores.

Into the ring
From various points away from any target, working either individually or in small groups, throw the beanbags into the container. How many successful attempts in three minutes?

Another version would be to place containers of different sizes at different points away from the starting places and to give different values for level of difficulty, eg the small yellow hoop 10 metres away from the starting place would score higher than the large red hoop 8 metres away.

Include a score card in the diagrams for children to record individual or group achievements.

Sports days

Childrens' athletic achievements can be celebrated in different ways. Many schools have tried organising their sports days to involve all children in physical activity on the day. This has included all youngsters in athletic activities not simply the gifted ones being cheered on by the rest of the school. Teachers have found that in spite of some initial scepticism by those more used to a traditional approach to sports day, they have been very successful and enjoyed by all concerned.

Try this approach:

all children take part on the day and boys and girls work together in teams of mixed age range;

the inside lane of a 400 metre track is marked and all activities are organised outwards from this line;

at each station activities are clearly represented on boards and an adult supervises each activity ensuring that all the children are safe, have an opportunity to take part and scores are recorded;

any number of activities are organised – from eight to twenty works well if there is one team working on every station. Each activity station needs to be numbered clearly. You could have four teams working at each station competing against each other, in which case fewer stations might be more practical;

spectators who are likely to be parents and friends (as all children are involved in activities) could be in the centre of the area or follow their team around the circuit;

timing is central and the timekeeper indicates the start by using a large cymbal, five minutes are given to each activity with two minutes for the change over;

have at least two stations where children have a short break and a drink if necessary.

Any activities which children have performed during the term could be included, but, as all age groups will be involved, keep them simple. Here is a bank of suggestions.

RUNNING ACTIVITIES
1. Run with a baton or quoit around a cone or mark on the ground and back. How many times can the whole team complete the course?
2. A 10-metre dash shuttle relay. How many times can the team return to the original formation?
3. Team star sprint. Take turns to run and touch the points of a star shape. How many 'stars' can the team complete in the time?
4. Hurdle squares. Set up two squares; two children at a time run around the squares, running freely over the hurdles. All children in the group take turns. How many circuits can the team complete?

Left: **Children at White Waltham School warming up for PE outdoors.**

Middle left: **A variety of markings on the playground at Calshot JS, Birmingham, gives scope for many games, physical activities and exercises. Space can be used by children at playtime and will inspire teachers and children in PE lessons too.**

Above and bottom left: **A colourful parachute can go up ... and down! There are many games and activities that can be enjoyed using parachutes. Several suggestions are made in the book, and teachers and children will be able to think up even more.**

Above and right: **Olympic Day at Coombes School, Arbourfield, Reading and the medal ceremony.**

Below: **Fun and exercise with hoops and rings at St Benedict's JS, Birmingham**

Below and right: **Children at White Waltham dancing round the maypole as children have done for generations.**

Above: **Yeobury Primary School, London's engine provides an interesting and imaginative place to play adventurously.**

Above and left: **The climbing wall at Kilmore Primary School, London**

Centre Left: **Camping out in the school grounds at Langley PS, Manchester.**

Left: **Swinging on a Jungle Gym at Barnaby JS, London is fun and healthy exercise as well. This is a particularly good activity for developing upper body strength. Children could match or contrast each other's shapes and movements.**

Above: **The main dancers for the Air section of th**
Firedance. (Francesca Neville and Nicola Dalai

Below: **`Old meets new´ the following year:**
Nicola Dalais from Riverdance and Carly
Bawden from Lord of the Dance.

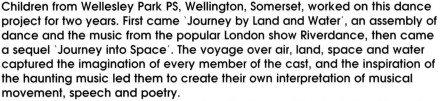

Children from Wellesley Park PS, Wellington, Somerset, worked on this dance project for two years. First came `Journey by Land and Water´, an assembly of dance and the music from the popular London show Riverdance, then came a sequel `Journey into Space´. The voyage over air, land, space and water captured the imagination of every member of the cast, and the inspiration of the haunting music led them to create their own interpretation of musical movement, speech and poetry.
Top: **The full cast in the opening number, Reel around the Sun in the Air section.**
Above: **Bicycle race in the Land section dance number 1.**
Below: **The A–Z of Space in the drama/comedy sketch of the Space section.**
The girl wearing a mortar board (Rebecca Warren) was the teacher and is holding the `naughty´ pupil (Jimmy Woodbury) by the ear.

5. Dribbling slalom. Use feet and football, or a hockey stick and light ball to dribble around three cones and back.

THROWING ACTIVITIES

1. Throw quoits or small hoops over cones or posts in the ground.
2. Throw a ball for distance. Put markers at various distances, eg past the blue mark scores 5, past the yellow 10, etc. Add up each individual's best throw for the team score.
3. Throw underarm into targets which have different values. Add up team scores.
4. Throw a frisbee as far as possible into space. Add up the team scores.
5. Throw beanbags overarm to targets on walls, fences or markings on the playground. Add up successful throws at hitting the target for team scores.

JUMPING ACTIVITIES

1. In groups of three or four, on four mats arranged longways, jump as far as you can as a team effort. The first person has three jumps and a line is drawn on the mat at the furthest score, which is the starting place for the next person to have three tries. Best jump is indicated by a line, and so on.
2. Skipping activity. Each child in the group skips and one point is recorded for every 25 uninterrupted skips recorded. Children may choose any skipping pattern.
3. Jump over canes or ropes at different heights. Simple scores allocated for different heights.
4. Combine two types of jumps to score a distance. For example hop and step: two footed jump and stride. Record the furthest distance and add up group scores.
5. Jump over outstretched ropes or lines to which different values have been allocated, for example parallel lines arranged at different distances, V shapes.

OTHER ACTIVITIES

1. Skip individually on the spot or around a marker and back.
2. Children form a line and hold hands. Pass a hoop along the line without breaking the line.
3. Mini obstacle maze. Run around a short course over one layer of the box, through a tunnel, under a rope supported by skittles, through hoops and skip back to finish. Younger children could run with older children.

4. Aim badminton shuttles into a bucket.
5. Group skipping activity. How many can skip in the long rope together?

OPPORTUNITIES FOR ALL TO SUCCEED

If this method of organising the sports day does not appeal you might consider a pattern which many schools have found to be popular with all concerned and is a combination of this and more traditional methods. Children who wish to run, jump and throw and compete in the more traditional activities do so in the morning, or on another day, and their scores are added to their team total for the next event which involves everybody.

OLYMPIC THEME

This theme adds another dimension to the occasion and works well. Children can design banners to represent their team and form a parade to and from the field. Inviting a sports celebrity to present the certificates or prizes also helps to make this a special occasion.

CHILDREN'S PLANNING

As children should be given credit and responsibility for planning in PE, organising sports day can be a very exciting project for them. At Newsham First School in Blyth Northumberland organising the Sports day for the whole school was the problem solving exercise set for the Year 2 class. The process has been described in more detail by Hornsey (1991). Children selected the activities, gave them names, devised record sheets, organised invitations, planned and served the refreshments and had a wonderful time learning across many areas of the curriculum.

A skipping activity.

Games

The Programme of Study for games classifies games into invasion, net, and striking/fielding games. There are numerous resources to help teachers to plan mini and modified versions of the main classification of games. Each governing body of sport provides advice and the Youth Sport Trust launched the 'Top Play'and 'Top Sports' programme which is in use in many primary schools.

Traditionally the school grounds have mostly been used for invasion games such as football and netball, with rounders being popular in the summer. Don't forget that there also many other exciting games, some traditional, which can delight children and form a worthwhile part of the programme and which also fulfil the requirements of the National Curriculum (see Resource List page). Many of these enable children to practise and refine the skills necessary for taking part in the more traditional forms of major games.

Creating games

When playing freely children improvise, adapt and create games which are fun and exciting. They use space imaginatively, often with limited equipment. Play is sometimes fiercely competitive and other times, without prompting, cooperative in nature. They make up names for their games, devise their own rules and boundaries, and keep to them. These are skills which children already have and ones which can be further developed in PE lessons at both Key Stages. Giving children opportunities to plan and devise their own games, either working alone, with a partner or in a small group, will enable them to take some responsibility to plan and then to evaluate their own performance. However, simply asking children to make up a game is not enough. Teachers need to ensure that the activities are worthwhile and safe. With appropriate guidance, children can create games which relate to the overall scheme of work for games and yet are unique to them. You might try the following approach:

Ask children to work in small groups and make up simple games using features in the grounds as targets. Examples of targets are tunnels, markings on the ground, walls or fences, posts, trees, skittles positioned on mounds. The task might be: select one or two items of equipment to send to the target (bean bags, quoits, balls of various sizes, hoops, discs, frisbees). The game must involve everyone being busy and active and it must be a challenging one. If the children are successful at hitting the target regularly, they should try to make the game more challenging for themselves. How can they do this? (Select a smaller target in the grounds, or move further away.) (See worksheet on page 51.)

CREATE A CLASS BOOK OF GAMES

Use the computer to produce a book of children's own games which will help the children to recognise that their contribution is valued. The book can then be used in subsequent lessons or used at playtime. The children will feel proud that other children are able to enjoy games which they have created.

Marking the area for games
GAMES USING CIRCLES

Six circles of the same size (the size doesn't matter as long as they are uniform) painted on the playground or marked on the field with enough space between to allow a good margin for safe skipping, hopping, running or chasing can be used for a variety of activities. If each is numbered it will make organisation smoother. Markings or numbers at regular intervals around the circle will also help children to find their spot quickly.

Here are some ideas for games which include five or six children in a group playing in a circle.

Pop goes the weasel
Five children hold hands and form a ring around the circle with the other child as 'the

Marking areas for games – six circles of the same size painted on the ground with enough space between them to allow a good margin for safety.

weasel' inside. In addition two or three extra weasels are nominated; they are not part of a circle but are positioned together in the middle of the area. On a signal, children dance in a circle around their weasels singing the nursery rhyme, 'Half a pound of two penny rice, half a pound of treacle. That's the way the money goes. Pop! goes the weasel!' On 'Pop!' all the weasels, including the extra ones, try to find another circle. As there are more weasels than circles different 'extra' weasels emerge and the game continues. This is a good game for large groups of young children.

Catch me if you can!
This game is safer on dry grass than the playground and requires a large circle for safety. As children are eliminated as the game progresses it would be a good choice for a concluding activity.

Children are widely and evenly spaced out around a circle all facing the same way. On a signal, they all run around the outside of the circle attempting to touch the person in front of them. When touched, that child is eliminated and runs out of the circle to stand at the side. The aim is to tag as many people as possible

without being tagged. In a more difficult version, after the start of the game the teacher blows a whistle to signify a change in direction and all change and chase in the opposite direction. To make this game enjoyable for all, children could be grouped around the circles in running ability.

Blobs
Small circles painted on the playground are ideal for this game which is best played in a small group. Children run across space and may jump from circle to circle. One or more catchers try to tag players when they are not in a circle. Any player standing in a circle must move on when another comes to take their place. It works well if played at a fast pace. Anyone tagged becomes a tagger.

Circle gap passing
Equipment: a large foam ball for each team.
This game will particularly benefit from markings around the circle for children to stay in place.

One player, A, is in the centre with the others spaced out evenly around the circle. A throws the ball to B who returns it to A and then runs behind C to receive it again in the gap between C and D , players C, D, E and F remain stationery. B throws it back and then receives through the next gap and so on until s/he returns to the original place. A then throws the ball to C who runs around the same way, sending and receiving the ball through the gaps in a similar way. Each player in the circle takes their turn. The first team in which each child completes their turn and sends the ball back to the player in the middle wins the contest.

A game of catch in a circle.

Circle gap passing.

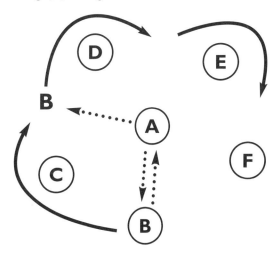

Circle dodge ball
Equipment: 2 large foam balls.
Six players are positioned around the outside of a circle with two players inside. Children on the circle throw the ball and attempt to hit the inside players on the legs with it. Encourage quick throwing and accurate fielding. The children on the inside of the circle may dodge, jump and run about freely to avoid being hit but must not move outside the line of the circle. When hit, the inside player changes places with the thrower. The winner is the player with the highest number of successful hits. Another way of scoring is to see who can remain for the longest time in the middle without being hit.

Guard the skittle
Children are arranged around the circle with one child in the middle guarding the skittle. The circle players throw a foam ball in an attempt to knock the skittle over. Encourage them to work as a team passing the ball between them to try to get it behind the guard. The person who knocks down the skittle changes places with the guard.

Stride ball
Children spread out around the circle with feet astride on the line. The aim is to roll the ball accurately between the legs of any other player except those on either side of the person with the ball. Players may prevent the ball from going through their legs by using their hands. If the feet of the 'target' player are moved, or the sender is successful, a point is scored by the sender. After a 'goal' is scored the person who let the ball through takes possession.

Pass the ball around the world
This is a throwing and catching game to encourage passing and moving. Children are positioned on the compass points with one child in the middle. A player on the outside passes to the centre player and follows the pathway of the ball into the centre. The centre player catches the ball and throws it to the next player on a compass point and follows the ball to take that player's place. Repeat, so that all players receive the ball. Children need to be alert and quick to move to the right place after they have sent the ball.

Corner spry
Equipment: a ball of any size or bean bag for each

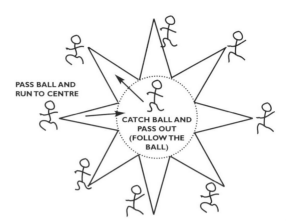

Pass the ball around the world.

team. This game can be played by throwing, kicking or passing the ball with a hockey or shinty stick.

Children number themselves 1–6. Players numbered 2–6 stand in a line facing number 1. On a signal player number 1 sends the ball to number 2 who returns it quickly. This is repeated down the line, each player receiving and returning it in turn. When the ball is received by number 6 s/he does not return it but runs with the ball to take the place of number 1 who moves across to the position of number 2. All other players move down a place. The game continues until all have had a go at each position and have worked their way back to their original places.

Using small areas

Walls of buildings in small corners of the playground also provide good areas for games using either freestanding targets or figures marked on the wall, providing that is, there is not a classroom on the other side! The walls each side of passageways can provide a useful 'tunnel' for rolling balls and aiming activities.

Placing mats in passageways will provide an area for jumping activities which do not require a run-up.

Games using targets

Walls, planks and fences act as good barriers for aiming games using freestanding targets. Targets set in front of them may include skittles, boxes, cones, larger balls or stumps. If there is enough space in the grounds a whole class can be busy creating individual or small group target games, sending balls or beanbags to hit their

Children playing corner spry.

have several attempts at the target. Use a stop-watch to see who is the quickest on each contest.

Knock the apples out of the tree

Using the tree markings, children throw bean bags hard over-arm to try to hit as many targets as possible in one minute. The target can be small balls sitting on the numbered circles within the tree. A partner can work coopera-tively to replace the target. Add up the scores of the value of the 'apples' which have been displaced. Start lines on the ground can be marked in different colours to indicate various levels of difficulty, so that the further away the thrower is from the target the higher the score. If the player throws from the nearest line to the targets, the scores are as read; how-ever if the throw is from the second line the scores are doubled; third line scores are trebled and so on.

targets. The barriers are useful in containing the balls and act as rebound boards which can also be incorporated into the games.

Number challenges

Add, subtract, multiply and divide the total of numbers scored by hitting the targets. For example, children work in pairs in competition to match, or double the score of their partner.

These kinds of activities will give children opportunities to practise and improve their aiming and sending skills and will also rein-force their mathematical skills. They can have some fun devising their own number games.

Wipe it out

Using a numbered fan grid, player A throws six bean bags to try to accumulate a high score. The number of each throw is totalled and then player B attempts to match the score exactly. The second player does not have to throw the bean bags on the same numbers.

One hundred and eighty!

Using a dart board design, children attempt to score 180 with the fewest number of throws. This can be an individual activity trying to improve effort, or played with children in competition with a partner, or between groups.

What's the time?

Children play in pairs. One decides and calls out a time and the other has to throw two bean bags to land on the appropriate numbers, eg 'quarter past twelve' – 12 and 15. Change roles and add up the number of successful throws. This can be played with a time penalty. Each child may

Snakes and ladders can be played on a board marked in the playground.

Animal magic

Animal shapes, for example giraffes, hippos, snakes and turtles with numbers or different colours painted on them, will inspire children to make up games. Challenges could include: How quickly can you score 50 by hitting the targets? Can you throw red bean bags to land on red colours, etc? Make up a jumping game using the shapes as targets.

Shooting goals

Children love scoring goals and if goal mouths are painted on walls they will spend endless time during play times trying to better their own performance. During games lessons they will enjoy trying to beat their own records and perfecting their technique. Play in pairs, threes and small groups will be more exciting if they have proper goals to attack and defend. Games can include kicking, rolling, throwing or sending the ball with a stick.

Games from long ago

Board games

Large checkerboards painted on the playground make great designs for games. Large foam dice can be thrown to indicate the number of moves and children move along pathways as if they are the pieces. For example, if the board is painted as a ludo board, teams can compete with each other in a attempt to get 'home' as in the parlour game. Movements may include stepping, hopping, jumping. Rules can be made up, for example whilst waiting on a square, players have to adopt a particular shape – wide, narrow, high or low, or balance on 1, 2, 3 or 4 parts of the body. If two players land on the same square they must find a way of balancing together. If a player needs to pass another on the journey around the board, the player who occupied the spot initially has to make a high or low shape for the other either to go over by leap frog or bunny jump. For safety: remind children making the shapes to support themselves with hands on knees to make a strong back and to tuck heads tightly in.)

Snakes and ladders

A good stimulus for playground games which need only foam dice as equipment is the game of snakes and ladders. The traditional design, however, ie up the ladders and down the snakes, can be adapted to suit the children who always have an opinion about best designs. Dalbeattie Primary School reported the fun had by all the primary 6 and 7 children devising designs such as 'up the school ruler and down the school ties', 'up the shooting stars and down the crescent moon' and even 'up the chips and down the tomato sauce'. They eventually decided on this design for their 'Snakes and ladders' type game (See page 35).

Hopscotch

Equipment: disc (a unihoc puck works well), a bean bag or stone.

Hopscotch is an old favourite and can be played alone or as a team. The disc can be kicked with the hopping foot (this is quite a difficult skill and might need free practice

Below: **There are many games associated with skipping. Here are children in Victorian dress playing one of them.**
Right: **Hopscotch has been played for many years.**

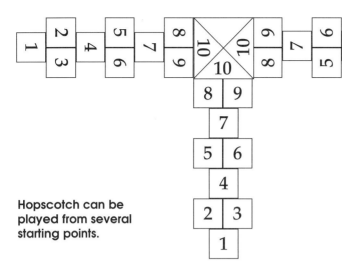

Hopscotch can be played from several starting points.

start line in as few attempts as possible. For example, if kicking has been selected for aiming and the first shot from behind the line is successful, the player attempts the next 'hole'. If, however, the puck does not land on the space, the player follows up the shot by hopping to the puck and then counts the number of attempts s/he takes before successfully landing on the target. Take turns, the player to complete the course in the fewest number of kicks, pushes/throws is the winner.

before the game is played) or the bean or stone is thrown onto the first square. The player moves up the hopscotch grid, hopping on the single squares and placing two feet on the double squares, avoiding the square containing the disc or beanbag. S/he then travels back along the grid picking up the object when it is reached. The disc, bean bag or stone is then sent to number 2 square and the sequence is repeated until the player reaches number 10 or misses the target square.

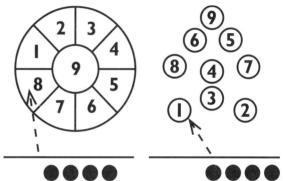

Hop-scotch golf
Equipment: uni-hoc stick and puck, or bean bags or quoits.

The object of this game is to kick a disc, push a disc with a stick or throw a quoit or beanbag into a series of marked spaces from behind a

Juggling
Children enjoy juggling balls or quoits in the air or against a wall. Individual challenges, eg how many items? how many times? or group marathons will encourage children to practise and refine their skills.

Games using imaginative themes
Themes in school grounds will stimulate children to invent their own active games, both in PE lessons and in their own time.

Permanent structures such as boats, ships or lighthouses accompanied by markings depicting treasure stores, islands, palm trees, fishes, whales, dolphins, rocks, pebbles and waves will encourage children to be active at playtime and in their PE lessons. Other themes such as farmyards with sheep pens, pigsties, cowsheds, milking parlour, grain stores, vehicle stores and open fields will open up other opportunities for nursery and very young children at Key Stage 1, as will the world of space travel. Children will come alive in these settings and will never fail to surprise you with their ideas!

You might consider asking your children for their ideas for developing the grounds along similar thematic lines.

Snakes and Ladders

100	99	98	97	96	95	94	93	92	91
81	82	83	84	85	86	87	88	89	90
80	79 78	77	76	75	74	73	72	71	
61	62	63 64	65	66	67	68	69 70		
60	59	58	57	56	55 54	53	52	51	
41	42	43 44	45	46	47	48	49	50	
40	39	38 37	36	35	34	33	32	31	
21	22	23 24	25	26	27	28	29	30	
20	19	18	17 16	15	14	13	12	11	
1	2	3	4 5	6	7	8	9	10	

Imaginative backgrounds and markings can stimulate children to make up their own games.

Designing small sided activities

It is relatively inexpensive to mark playing areas with lines and boxes which will make the world of difference for teachers and children in PE lessons. When considering the size and shape of the playing areas, give consideration to the number of children involved, their sizes and their levels of ability. Giving grids a number or colour will make management of order easier for the teacher when organising apparatus and groups of children. If spaces are identified, some of the organisation can be explained to the children before they leave the classroom. This will provide children with a place and a defined boundary which will help in all physical activities.

The most adaptable markings for both playground and grassed areas are grid squares.

The most flexible size is 10 m x 10 m. These are especially valuable for small group activities leading towards invasion games and net games which can then be combined to enable children to play small sided games against each other. A block of 6 x 4 grids will give teachers maximum opportunities to set up a variety of games situations to suit the experience and ability of the children and also to observe all the games in action. A line down the centre of a playground marked with a netball court will provide six working grid areas.

See DfEE (1996) for regulations about school playing fields or equivalent sporting facilities which apply to any school where there are pupils aged eight years or above.

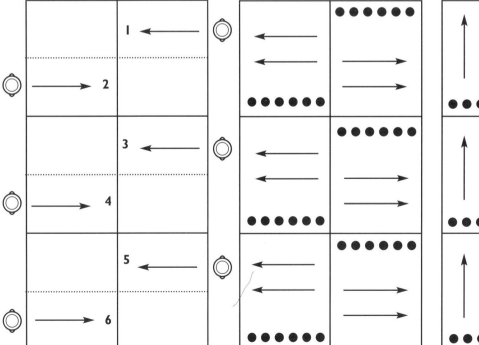
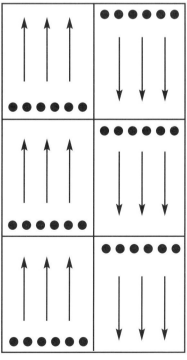

Some suggestions for class organisation on a netball court.

Dance

Dancing outdoors on a fine day can be really exhilarating. The school grounds can provide wonderful performance spaces for dance. This might be simply a piece of flat ground or a turf mound amphitheatre created especially as a performance space. Features of the landscape and scenery can provide the stimulus for ideas. The feel of soft grass underfoot, different shapes, levels and textures may stimulate children's creative ideas. The school playground may be used as a venue for traditional folk dances on fine days and a dance event could be organised to enable children, parents and friends in the community to meet and dance together.

Encourage the children to compose their own accompaniment to their dances using percussion instruments. Being outside can often be less restricting than the hall because you will not have to worry about the noise imposing on other classrooms. Chanting word rhythms, clapping, using poetry, sounds from the environment or even silence can provide effective accompaniments for dance.

Stimuli for Dance in the Grounds

VISUAL
Leaves falling, turning and settling;
Ash or sycamore keys twisting, twirling, spinning and whirling;
Shape and movement of trees and shrubs changing in the breeze;
Colours, mixed and separate, for mood changes;
Lines, angles, shapes and skylines;
Sculpture;
Light and shade;
Animals and mini-beasts;
Weather;
Seasons.

SOUNDS
Traffic;
Voices;
Birds;
Aeroplanes;
Silence.

TACTILE
Contrasts in shape and form, for example bark, pebbles, leaves, grass.

Harmony/disharmony, eg sand – concrete, ferns – wire, reeds – poles, bumpy – smooth, flat – undulating, steep – gentle slopes, dandelion clocks – teasles.

Bubbles blown into the open space can delight young children and provide a starting point for dance (if you can discourage them from simply running after them).

PLACES
Hide and seek has been enjoyed by children throughout the ages in different forms. In spacious school grounds it lends itself nicely to being developed as a dance idea. Of course, it

Natural features can be a stimulus for making up dance movements (left) and places to hide (right).

will be necessary to set limits and boundaries and initially the ideas will need to be developed in a restricted area. As a dance it will be more controlled than as a 'free for all' recreational game.

Children work in pairs (A and B) and each decides on a 'hiding place', for example, against a fence or a wall (they do not literally have to be hidden, but could be very still or adopt a shape and position to blend in with the surroundings) under a bush, in a shadow, behind a tree.

Dance Framework

Start with pupils A and B in harmonious positions together in open space; for example – leaning side by side, one high one low, facing each other, etc.

A indicates with a gesture that s/he is going to hide; B indicates with a gesture that s/he agrees.

A dances away and disappears to hiding place.

B covers eyes, waits rocking out a rhythm and calls 'Ready or not' and runs forwards and backwards on two different pathways searching.

B finds A.

A pops up when B goes down and they alternate until they are both at the same level and B 'finds' A.

Roles are then changed.

B dances away and A waits for a moment and the sequence is repeated.

Both return to the original position.

This dance idea will provide lots of fun for children who are used to creating their own dances, who relish the opportunity to create rhythms and sounds to accompany their dances and want to create something different.

'Tarmac and concrete is boring, like seeing a film ten times.'

THEN AND NOW

Changes over time to the school grounds make a wonderful starting point for dance. You might consider using photographs of your own grounds similar to those below.

Ask children to look at the photographs and say how they make them feel.

Identify the action words suggested by the photographs (they will need to look at the original).

Take each action word in turn and explore the movement ideas as a class activity.

Work in pairs and select the actions which best represent how they feel personally about the environment as it was and is now.

The dance would be about contrasts in emotions and feelings. The same photographs could also be used as starting points to develop contrasts in opportunities for physical play.

Children will need plenty of time to explore, select, rehearse and refine their ideas and have the opportunity to watch each other's dances and make comments on what they see.

Look at the photographs (if a photograph from the past is not available you might use a painting by Bruegel as the stimulus for example, *Children's Games*). Discuss the differences in

'This school is very, very interesting and we're very happy here.'

Left: **A corner of the Coombes Infants, Aborfield grounds can be used as a performance space for the children or visiting actors.**
Below: **Children from St Michael's, Bristol, use a space for an impromptu performance.**

the dress and expressions on children's faces.

Talk about the games and activities which they might enjoy at playtime.

The movement from the games ideas could be developed into dance. Children should not literally play the games, but select some action words which best represent the activity for example, hop scotch: hop, step, jump; skate boarding: slide, jump, turn. Children need to make these actions larger than life and then develop them into a rhythmic pattern.

A suggested framework for the dance

The dance begins with the children in small groups posing as in the photograph below.

In pairs or groups of three they move out of the poses and travel into a different space.

As though travelling through time they travel by turning steps back to the original starting spot to form a second group pose symbolic of the more modern pose.

In their same small groups they perform a different dance to represent present day activities.

At the end of the dance they regroup as one of the photograph poses.

Using the grounds as a performance space

Example: the journey.

Children from Wellesley Park School, Wellington, Somerset under direction of their class teacher Roger Hitchin created magical dances based around a journey over air, land, space and water. The success of their production inspired other dance productions stimulated by the shows *River Dance* and *Lord of the Dance*. The pieces also involved singing, instrumental soloists, sketches, poetry. The enthusiasm of the children was electric. They loved performing their dances outside. The different levels of the terrain provided the perfect stage and the backdrop of the blossom and vegetation complemented the colours of their costumes.

An outdoor performance of Edward Lear's poem, 'The Owl and the Pussy Cat' at Wellesley Park Primary School.

A Chinese dragon dance

Children's feelings as stimulus for dance

Children will enjoy creating dances inspired by their concerns about their school environment. For example dance can be created from issues arising from changes in use of the grounds, the natural things that live there, or negative signs, eg litter/rubbish/vandalism.

Research has shown that children have very strong views about the care and maintenance of the school grounds and are generally distressed by places which are a mess. Often they regard acts of vandalism and damage to the school as direct attacks on themselves.

'People vandalise the school because they're jealous. It makes us annoyed and angry and upset. It makes the place look so awful from the outside' (WWF/LTL 1994, p 52).

Children's views on these issues can be expressed through dance. The above quotation could be used as the stimulus for the dance. Ask children:

How does it make you feel when people vandalise the grounds?

What actions best express anger? annoyance? (Examples: gestures such as stamping, punching, kicking, shrugging, pointing).

How do people move when they are upset?

In small groups create a dance which expresses your feeling towards vandalism.

The grounds could be the perfect setting for a performance in which the children are given the opportunity to express their feelings on this issue through dance, raps, chants, music, poetry and drama.

ENVIRONMENTAL ART

Many people will be familiar with the work of Andy Goldsworthy (see, for example, *Parkland* by Goldworthy 1988) who uses natural elements to create art in the environment. This work could be the stimulus for childrens' art work in the grounds and could lead on to dance. Children's understanding of how shape form and space are presented can be enhanced through this art form. Spiral structures lend themselves particularly well to dance or contrasting textures of the materials could be the starting point. Children can create, perform, and view dances which have been composed from this stimulus. Children might work on floor patterns and aerial pathways using their own art work as inspiration.

CELEBRATION AND FESTIVALS

Dances of celebration work well outdoors. Children could create music and dance for a Chinese dragon dance, a dance to celebrate the festival of Diwali, or a samba through the school grounds.

FOLK DANCES

Folk dances from all around the world are better performed on the playground or field than in the hall. Most folk dances are well suited to the outdoor environment and performed with others at festival times. All dances, whatever their origin, involve people forming patterns, eg lines, circles, star shapes and rectangles and simple symmetry. Markings on the ground can help young children to find a place at the beginning of their dances. Fun can be had with line formations, for example dancing traditional dances from Brittany which involve meandering around the grounds as the dancers do through the towns and villages during festivals in France. Circle dances are very exciting; they may begin as an open circle leaving a space for others to join in and then turn into a snaky shapes, spirals or a labyrinth shapes. Many European dances include these figures.

Asian dances, African dances and dances from the Americas can all be performed outside and enjoyed by those participating and others watching. Children could be encouraged to make up dance steps and create their own formations which suit the available space.

Maypole dancing is often a feature of the May celebrations. You might also consider encouraging children to create dances around trees or bushes in your grounds.

Tape recorders and CD players can be taken outside for the accompaniment. However children will love acting as the band for their best known dances. A larger space might enable several classes to dance together and could be combined with some singing breaks. (See Upton and Paine, 'Up the Sides and Down the Middle' for a variety of English folk dances.)

ARTISTES IN RESIDENCE
Invite professional dancers or parents in to work with the children in the grounds. Most dance companies have an education department and will be delighted to send someone into the school to teach children an aspect of their forthcoming dance production, a particular technique or dance from different times or cultures. This can be combined with other Arts events or to celebrate School Grounds Week.

DANCE DRAMA
Shipwrecks, earthquakes, mountain rescue and forest adventures are easily created outside using the natural features of the grounds such as mounds, dips, valleys, ridges, woods, as a stage for the activities. The environment will enhance the drama, but it does need sensible control to be successful. The movement possibilities and boundaries can be planned in the classroom and the dance drama designed piece by piece. Refining work in pairs and small groups will be necessary to prevent chaos in the freedom of the space. Battles are fantastic outside when the rules of combat and chivalry are respected!

OBSERVING MOVEMENT

A framework to develop movement qualities in dance and gymnastic activities. When observing movement as a teacher remember that these aspects are important.

TIME:
remember that actions can be:
    fast/slow;
    sudden/sustained accelerating/decelerating;
    rhythmical.

SPACE:
remember that movement can be performed in personal space and in general space with others;
    at high, medium or low levels;
    in different directions – forwards, backwards, sideways;
    along different pathways – direct, indirect, straight or curving.

CONTINUITY:
remember whatever the speed and force of the movement:
    it should be controlled;
    transitions from one action to the next should be smooth.

FORCE:
remember that actions can be:
    heavy/light.

Gymnastic Activities

Children think that performing gymnastic activities on the grass is brilliant! Of course it does require a fine day, dry grass and an enthusiastic teacher to make it a success. It also requires some careful thought as to the organisation and equipment. High quality work can be achieved outside. Schools with limited hall space can enable children to enjoy their gymnastic activities programme in the grounds when the weather is fine.

Safety

Check that the grass is dry, the day is warm and that the ground is not rock hard from continuous hot weather.

Remember that running and chasing games across the apparatus are dangerous and should not be played.

Provide children with mats to work on.

Teach children to carry and place portable apparatus such as benches and box tops and solid box bottoms safely. (Choose an area close to the store if possible so that children have less far to move the apparatus.)

Remember that high, light agility tables are unstable on grass.

Equipment

Ropes and canes supported by skittles will provide children with apparatus to move under, around or over.

Climbing and swinging activities using the fixed outside climbing equipment will fulfil National Curriculum requirements of climbing, hanging and swinging. It will also have a positive effect on children's upper body strength. Suspended tyres to swing on, logs to climb, rails to turn over and hang from can be enjoyed by children of all ages. A scrambling net as part of a trail tests strength and confidence.

Logs, bars and planks can be used in addition to portable gymnastic apparatus for balancing and travelling activities.

Planning

A whole school approach to planning themes for gymnastics activities is necessary to challenge children at their level of achievement. A range of resources is available to help schools to plan schemes of work that are progressive. Some of these are listed on pages 53 and 54.

Themes which are most commonly taught at Key Stage 1 and 2 include:
Travelling on feet, hands and feet;
Using personal and general space;
Taking weight and balancing on different parts of the body;
Jumping and landing with control;
Body shape – stretched, curled, symmetrical and asymmetrical, rolling, twisting and turning.

Supporting weight on hands and arms to make a symmetrical shape.

Any of these themes could be be taught in the grounds. A gentle grassy slope can be used for rolling activities. The climbing and swinging apparatus can be used in a gymnastics context. On a sunny day children could have some fun matching each others' shadow shapes as a starting point to their sequences.

The lesson plan would be similar to the indoor lesson. Teachers need to position themselves on the outside of the designated space looking inwards so that all children can be observed. As with the indoor lesson there will be tasks set for the whole class and children should have the opportunity to explore their individual responses, plan their own sequences and watch and comment on the work of others.

If a range of apparatus is available, the groups should rotate so that children have the opportunity to refine their movements on a variety of apparatus. However, if no apparatus is available, good quality work can be achieved in floor work activities on mats.

Task cards will be very helpful when working outside. For a super range of task cards suitable for the upper primary age group see

Agile (Underwood, 1991). These have pictorial images of gymnastic activities and will enable children to work independently in the grounds.

Balance and shape

Any school grounds will have natural or manmade objects with either wide or narrow bases and these can be a stimulus for gymnastic activities. Examples are endless and might include logs, trees, walls, benches, swings, climbing frames, bird tables, sundials, sculptures, gates, or buildings.

LARGE BASES
Suggest that the children identify something which they can see which has a wide base.

Ask them to decide on the body parts which will best support them.

Ask them to make these shapes and be very stretched and still and then to move very smoothly from one shape to the next, for example by rocking or rolling.

BRIDGE SHAPES
A lot of fun can be had making bridge shapes balancing on small bases, eg hands, feet, heads, knees and shoulders. Ask children to find different ways of linking these shapes, for example by turning the body from one shape to another at different speeds.

This can be further developed in pairs with one child making a strong, still bridge shape with plenty of space underneath. Without touching the other person, the partner finds two different ways of going underneath and

Children in balance positions.

around the shape. Children take turns to make the bridge shape.

This can be developed by adding linking movements to make longer sequences.

Beginning with one movement balance on large or small bases:

(i) turn in to another shape;
(ii) twist into another shape;
(iii) roll into another shape.

Symmetrical and asymmetrical shapes

Ask children to look at the shapes of objects and features in the grounds and to say whether they are symmetrical or asymmetrical. Suggest that they work alone, in pairs or small groups and make matching shapes with their bodies. Remind them about good body shape and tension. Working on soft grass, mats, bars and climbing frames, children will enjoy making shapes together and finding creative ways of linking their movements with rolls, twists and turns, moving in and out of balance.

Ask children to compose sequences which include either travelling, jumping, landing or rolling, using symmetrical or asymmetrical shapes and ending in symmetrical or asymmetrical balances.

Suggest that they work alone, then with a partner, and if that works well, in a group of three or four.

Perform:

(i) on the mat;
(ii) on the low apparatus;
(iii) upside down;
(iv) in the air;
(v) on the climbing apparatus.

Encourage the children to evaluate their own work and the work of others and comment on the clarity of body shape (eg do the shapes match any which they see around them in the grounds?), the composition of the sequences and the quality of the transitions between one movement and the next.

Children in balance positions.

Outdoor Adventurous Activities

The school grounds can provide one of the safest places for outdoor and adventurous activities. Children will gain confidence and skills in a secure environment which they may be able to use later in less familiar surroundings. Working together and considering others is a focus of this programme of study. They will love obstacle courses, solving problems, exploring and investigating. For many, an overnight camp will be the highlight of the year.

Ropes, tyres, logs, trim trails, wooded areas and adventure playground equipment will inspire children to explore, experiment and challenge themselves and each other in a range of tasks. Many problem-solving activities require very little specialist equipment and simple activities will fulfil National Curriculum requirements. Much of the apparatus used for games and athletic activities may be used for Outdoor and Adventurous Activities.

For cross-curricular approaches at all stages of the National Curriculum, using the 'outdoor classroom', see a resource pack 'Outdoor and Environmental Education', produced by Manchester City Council (1993). This provides planning sheets for activity-based and thematic work across the whole curriculum.

Orienteering

There are different forms of orienteering, for example: cross-country, score orienteering where controls are given points value which reflect the degree of difficulty and distance from the start; line orienteering in which lines are drawn on a map marking a route which goes along or over an assortment of obstacles; and relays where children work in teams and trail events. All different forms of orienteering contain elements of navigation, decision making and physical activity.

These activities combine either walking, running or cycling with map work skills and will give children an opportunity to sharpen their observation skills and plan with others. They are good for fitness too!

There are many different courses which may be set out in the grounds.

Very practical books on orienteering activities are available and those looking for a variety of ideas for teaching orienteering should refer to McNeill, Ramsden and Renfrew (1987) and McNeill, Martland and Palmer (1992).

Cross-country

Cross-country orienteering requires children to follow a route and visit a number of control points in a set order. The best performance is by the person or team who find their way in the shortest time. You might consider setting up several routes around the school grounds to suit the age and ability of the children taking part.

Map reading to follow the green route in the school grounds.

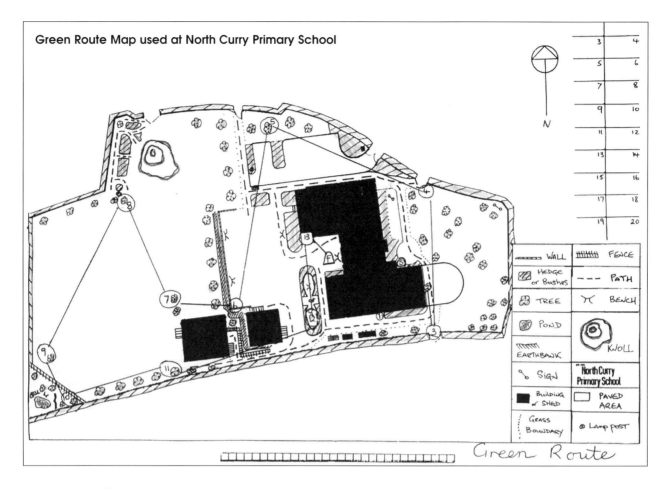

Green Route Map used at North Curry Primary School

WALL | FENCE
HEDGE or Bushes | PATH
TREE | BENCH
POND | KNOLL
EARTHBANK
SIGN | North Curry Primary School
BUILDING or SHED | PAVED AREA
GRASS BOUNDARY | LAMP POST

Green Route

Trails in the grounds

Trails are great fun to follow. All trails involve the children going on journeys and there are many ways of linking this work outdoors with other areas of the curriculum. Children can match words, find colours, collect things, identify sounds, or look for clues. Trails could be set to find historical or geographical features in the school grounds.

Map reading on a cross-country trail.

OBSTACLE TRAILS

Children can have fun designing their own obstacle trails using the adventure play equipment in the school grounds. Tyres, pipes, tunnels, benches, hoops, crates, boxes, rope and string may all be used to encourage children to climb, balance, crawl, swing, jump and land with control in challenging situations.

Of course it is vital that the trails are checked for safety and that rules are devised for each activity to ensure safe practice. There should be no chasing activity on such equipment.

STRING TRAILS

(Use strong string or cord approximately 50 metres long.)

Following a string trail which is attached to a tree, fence or post is another way of helping children to explore their environment. To add interest, clues, treasure, surprises, or information can be hung at high places along the way.

Children can record their findings in a variety of ways. They may wish to work independently or in pairs, following the string trail by keeping one hand on the string all the way. If one partner is blindfolded this idea can be further developed, but of course consideration needs to be given to safety.

Wild areas make perfect locations for these trails. Good use can be made of natural challenges such as stepping over logs, crawling under branches or squeezing through dense vegetation. If such features are lacking, include activities such as crawling through tunnels, barrels or under a tarpaulin to add to the challenge. It is best to keep the groups small with no more than ten children spaced out along the trail at the same time .

FINDING THE REAL THING
Take about 24 photographs including for example, flowers, trees, sides of buildings, climbing apparatus, drainpipes, gutters, notices, markings, pond life, shrubs and pathways. Back the photograph onto a firm fabric and give it a number on the back to identify the location.

This activity involves children recognising features in the school grounds, locating them on the base map and recording their positions on the map. They can work in pairs taking it in turns to lead the way.

TEXTURES
On a base map mark 16 places for the children to visit and number them 1–16 on the map. Each pair are given a base map, a wax crayon and a large sheet of paper which is divided into 16 squares. In each box provide a clue for the texture the children should look for at the specific location. Children place the paper over the surface and use the wax crayon to rub gently over the area to record an impression of the texture in the appropriate box. Inexperienced children can return to base each time for the teacher to check. Children who are more experienced complete the whole trail before returning to base.

Camp craft in the school grounds
Camping in the school grounds can be a real adventure. If it is possible for children to spend a night or two under canvas for some it will be the first time away from home.

Children can learn about suitable sites for tents and take some responsibility for choosing their own site. This will increase awareness of soil properties, the layout of the land and how

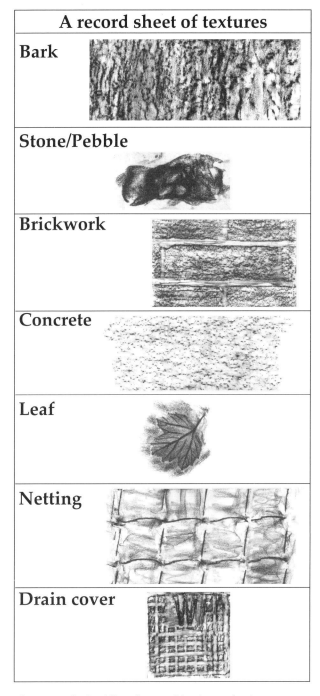

A record sheet of textures

Bark

Stone/Pebble

Brickwork

Concrete

Leaf

Netting

Drain cover

One way to feel the size and texture of a tree.

to find the best shelter from the elements. Planning the site, knowing how to be safe, selecting what to wear and choosing the menus is all part of staying outdoors. Erecting tents takes quite a lot of practice and children need to develop careful listening and observational skills. They also need to cooperate and get on well with each other to get it right. All sorts of scientific and mathematical concepts relating to properties, angles and shape can be reinforced. Once they know what to do, they will enjoy group challenges to see who can get ready first.

Living together, if only for a weekend, requires children to trust each other, share jobs and pay attention to hygiene. Many issues in relation to health education can be reinforced whilst engaging in these activities. Activities such as packing a rucksack and finding out how different materials respond in various weather conditions can be discovered in the familiar environment.

Camp fires can be special events and songs, some perhaps with action words, activities and stories can be planned and created by children and enjoyed during their stop over.

Most LEAs have guidelines on Outdoor and Adventurous Activities and the Scout Association and the Guide Association have both produced excellent publications which schools will find useful as guidance for camp craft.

Ropes

There are many challenging activities which can be enjoyed in the school grounds on tight ropes tied to trees or other suitable supports. Many include activities in a non-competitive way to promote team work. Whilst every course should be designed to be interesting for the children, safety of course is of primary importance. Rope courses and any trees they are attached to should be inspected annually and you might consider using hessian sacking to protect the trees. Contact the Advisory Association for Rope Courses and Initiatives (AARCI) for advice. Also consult CHSU-Guidance for Schools (1996) Vol 5 – 1.02 – Section 19 – Page 32 for safety guidance.

Problem solving activities

Co-operating with others and the development of decision-making skills and team-building skills is the essence of Outdoor and Adventurous Activities in the primary curriculum. Children will love working together to solve problems and enjoy testing themselves in a variety of challenging situations. Several different activities can be set up in the school grounds for children to work on in groups, moving from one to another. These activities could form part of a scheme of work.

A CAROUSEL OF ACTIVITIES

Children could work in small groups of six or eight for these activities; this will depend on the facilities and equipment.

Children are provided with two planks with

Camping out in the school grounds

slings or 12mm rope attached and the challenge is to get from point A to B in the grounds with all the team 'on board'. Tell them that they are allowed to have one team member directing operations from the side.

The group will have to work very much as a team as they have to keep both feet on the planks at all times and try to create a rhythm to move along together. You might increase the distance to be travelled or look for more difficult terrain for children experienced in this activity. Another way to make this more challenging is to give realistic time limits or see if the children can beat their own time record.

Spider's web

Equipment: a vertical web of rope attached across goal posts, or trees.

The aim of this activity is for the children to get the whole group through the spaces in the 'web' without touching the rope. Tell them to imagine that it is electric wire and they must get the whole team through without touching the wire.

Don't let 'em get you!

Crossing the infested swamp (children can invent all sorts of scenarios for this one).
Equipment: any 'stepping stones', eg. individual small mats, old swimming floats, strong crates or boarded crates or rubber quoits.

A marked-out wide river on the playground, level ground or a valley between slopes will provide the imaginary danger area for this one. The distance between boundaries can vary according to the size and ability of the children. The aim is to get all the group over the stepping stones without them putting their feet in the infested water.

It is important to have enough stepping stones for each of the group to stand on and one spare to pass from the back of the team to the front to enable them to progress. Ask them to find a way of getting everyone (and their stepping stones) to the other side. Once they have managed the task suggest that they try to speed it up to become more efficient each time.

A variation on the above activity is to have ropes or coloured tape tied to trees or posts to negotiate along the pathway, eg one at about half a metre for children to go underneath and another at one metre which children must go over.

The children will need to help each other to get across the swamp, over the rope and under the rope without falling in!

Sticking together in a knot

Equipment: Rope.

Show a small group of the children how to tie a reef knot or initially show them the diagram on page 50. Show them that a reef knot is tied by the ends of the rope going right over left and under, then left over right and under. Then pull the two ends to make a strong, flat knot. The task is for all the group to pick up the rope and, not letting go, together tie a reef knot around a tree. They need to think about both ends of the rope.

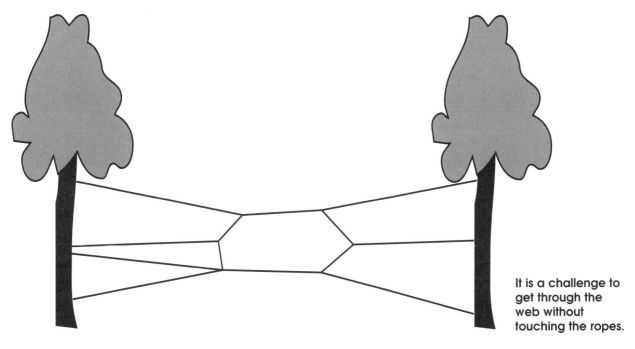

It is a challenge to get through the web without touching the ropes.

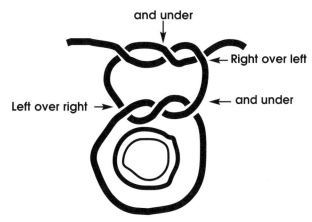

and under

Right over left

Left over right

and under

Tying a reef knot around a tree.

Dens and shelters

Shelters can be constructed from hazel rods, willow and other materials such as straw, clay, branches and leaves. (See *Arts in the School Grounds*). If there is a low wall in the school grounds this will be ideal for constructing a simple bivouac shelter. Give children a piece of material or a sheet and ask them to find ways of securing the top and bottom with large pebbles or stones so that they have made a roof for shelter. Dens can also be easily created in undergrowth.

Inventing games which involve sneaking up on 'enemy' camps has often been a focus of children's play and this can be developed in PE lessons. Suggest that two groups of four or five children each set up a den no further than fifty metres apart. Each team has two containers which they endeavour to smuggle into each other's dens. This is a non-contact activity so no tackling is allowed. A point system might be introduced for children spotted approaching their opponents' den, or children could race each other against the clock to see who accomplishes their mission first. Children are always very good at inventing their own rules for such ventures.

Hawkeye

If there is an area of long grass or bushes in an enclosed area that would be ideal for this activity. One child sits down in a predetermined area and the other children attempt to creep up on her/him, making use of local cover to hide. The aim is to get as close as possible to Hawkeye without being seen. Those who are spotted in the process of the stalk have to stand up and remain still until the time allotted for the game is up. The person who is the first to touch Hawkeye without being seen replaces him.

Teach the children some basic crawls which they might use in stalking each other through woodland and or long grass.

Kim's game

This is primarily a game of observation (inspired by Kipling) which can involve a small group working against time to identify objects, or children cooperating in pairs or teams to identify objects quicker than each other in competition. It is probably best planned as part of a series of group activities. It is fun but rather static, best played on a warm day.

You will need to prepare a master map of the area which has been marked with grids. On the map mark the exact spot when you have placed a number of items at different distances from the start line. These could be anything for example, ping pong balls, bean bags, whistles, swimming floats, canes, skipping ropes, or small balls of different colour. Section off an area or several identical areas (you might use vector shapes) and place clearly identifiable markers at intervals of 10, 20, 30, 40 metres away from the start line. The distance to be covered will depend on the age of the children. Use markers or rope on grass or tape or chalk if playing on tarmac to break up the area into grids. Each grid will need to be clearly identified with a letter, number or coloured flag.

Each group will be provided with a blank scaled map. Children must stay along the start line. One person in each group will be given a set of binoculars (you could ask children to bring them in). Each member in turn will be allowed a set period of observation (30 seconds). A second child will have the map and will mark in any objects seen. After the set period a whistle is blown and children change roles. The child with the map hands it to his/her friend behind and takes up the observation. A whistle blast starts the next sequence. This process continues until all children have had a period of observation. At the completion of the series each group hands its map to the teacher. These maps are then compared with the master map and points are allocated for objects identified. These are marked on a sliding scale, ie nearer/bigger objects score less than smaller objects far away.

Creating Target Games

CHALLENGE

Planning

Choose your equipment. This could be
a bean bag, a small ball, a large ball,
a bat and ball or a unihoc stick and ball.
Select a target for your game.
In pairs make up a simple scoring game
that involves aiming at the target.
Decide on your area of play. Agree any rules
before you start. How will you record the score?

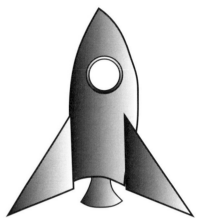

PLAY YOUR GAME TOGETHER

Is it exciting?
Could you do anything to make it better?
Do you need to change anything to
make it a better game?

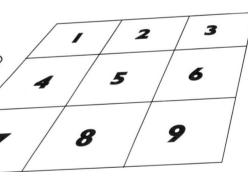

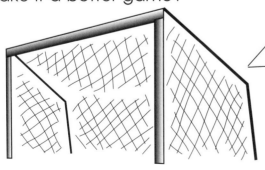

EVALUATING

Questions

Is it easier to hit a target when you are close or far away?
Is it easier to hit a big target or a small target?
Is it easier to hit a target with a small ball or a big ball?
Give your game a special name. Describe your
game to others in the class.

Health Related Exercise

Exercise Challenge
Measure your breathing rate and heart rate

Equipment: stop watch

Choose an activity that you enjoy doing, for example skipping with a rope, a running/chasing game, cycling, running the activity trail. Keep going for five minutes.

Measure your breathing rate and heart rate before and after exercise.

This is how you measure your breathing rate.

You will need a partner to time you with a stopwatch. Gently place your left hand flat on your tummy below your breast bone. Your tummy will rise and push against your hand when a breath is taken in and will fall when a breath is blown out. Watch this happening before you start your activity. Count the number of breaths in 15 seconds. Place your hand on your tummy and find the right spot. Your partner says, 'Ready and go' and starts the watch: 'One, two, three ... and stop' (after 15 seconds).
Record on the chart below.

This is how you measure your heart rate.

The heart rate can be measured by counting the pulse. To find your pulse gently place the first and second fingers of your right hand on your left wrist just below the wrist joint and opposite the first finger of the left hand, or find the pulse on the side of your neck, just below the jaw bone. Your partner says, 'Ready and go, one, two, three, four, five and stop' (after 6 seconds). Count the number of beats in six seconds and record it on the chart below. Add a nought to the figure to convert it into the number of beats per minute.

Breathing rate record sheet	
Name: _____	
Class: _____ Date: _____	
	Breathing rate/15 seconds
At rest	_____
After 3 minutes' warm-up	_____
After 3 minutes' activity	_____
After 6 minutes' activity	_____
After 9 minutes' activity	_____
After 12 minutes' activity	_____

Heart rate record sheet		
Name: _____		
Class: _____ Date: _____		
	Heart rate/6 secs	Heart rate/Min
At rest	_____	_____
After 3 minutes' warm-up	_____	_____
After 3 minutes' activity	_____	_____
After 6 minutes' activity	_____	_____
After 9 minutes' activity	_____	_____
After 12 minutes' activity	_____	_____

References and Resources

References

Balazik, D. *Outdoor and Adventurous Activities for Juniors.* A&C Black, 1995

Board of Education (1933) *Syllabus of Physical Training.* HMSO.

Bray, S. *Fitness Fun. Promoting Health in the Physical Education Programme.* Southgate, 1993

British Advisers and Lecturers in Physical Education (BAALPE), *Safe Practice in Physical Education.* BAALPE, 1996

CHSU Guidance for Schools. Vol 5, Vers 1.02, Section 19. ps 32–33.
Department for Education and Employment (DfEE). *The 1996 School Premises Regulations.* Circular 10/96. DfEE, 1996

Goldsworthy, A. *Parkland.* Bretton Hall College, 1988

Harris, J. and Elbourn, J. *Teaching Health Related Exercise at Key Stages 1 and 2.* Human Kinetics, 1997

The Scottish Office Education Department. *Curriculum and Assessment in Scotland National Guidelines Expressive Arts.* 5–14, HMSO Scotland, 1992

The Scottish Office Education Department. *Curriculum and Assessment in Scotland National Guidelines Environmental Studies.* 5–14, HMSO Scotland, 1993

Department for Education. *Key Stages 1 and 2 of the National Curriculum: Physical Education.* HMSO, 1995

Hertfordshire County Council (HES) *Games Activities in the Primary School.* HES, 1995

Hornsby, A. *Sports Day: A Cross Curricular Approach to Planning. Primary P.E. Focus,* pp. 11–12. Summer. 1991

Keighley, P.W.S. *Orientation at Key Stage 2. Primary P.E. Focus,* pp. 5–9. Spring. 1996

Lucas, W. Preface in W. Titman, *Special Places; Special People.* WWF/LTL, 1994

McNeill, C. Martland, J. and Palmer, P. (1992) *Orienteering in the National Curriculum. A Practical Guide.* Harveys, 1992

McNeill, C. Ramsden, J. and Renfrew, T. *Teaching Orienteering.* Harveys, 1987

McNeill, C. and Renfrew, T. *Start Orienteering Book 1 (6–8 year olds) Book 2 (8–9 year olds) Book 3 (9–10 year olds) Book 4 (10–12 year olds) Book 6 Games and Exercises.* Harveys, 1994

Outdoor and Environmental Education in the National Curriculum. Manchester City Council & Field Studies Council, 1993

Martin, B. Bancroft, G. Hore, M. and Roberts, G. *Outdoor and Adventurous Activities In Teaching Physical Education at Key Stages One and Two.* Physical Education Association, 1995

Titman, W. *Special Places; Special People.* WWF/LTL, 1994

Yesterday's Games Today. A Booklet.
Available from: National Centre for Play, Moray House Institute, Cramond Road, North Cramond Campus. Edinburgh EH4 6JD

Resources:
PHYSICAL EDUCATION FOR CHILDREN WITH SPECIAL EDUCATIONAL NEEDS

Brown, A. *Active Games for Children with Movement Problems*. Paul Chapman, 1987

Knight, E. and Chedzoy, S. *Physical Education in the Primary School. Access for All*. David Fulton, 1997

HEALTH RELATED EXERCISE
Sleap, M. and Hickman, J, *Fit for Life 1. Physical Activity Sessions for Children aged 4–9 years*. The University of Hull, Research Centre for PE, Exercise and Health, 1994

Sleap, M. Fit for Life 2. *Physical Activity Sessions for Children aged 7–13 years*. University of Hull, Research Centre for PE, Exercise and Health, 1994

Health Education Authority. *Happy Heart 1 Resources for 4 to 7 year olds*. Thomas Nelson, 1990

Health Education Authority. *Happy Heart 2. Resources for 7 to 11 year olds*. Thomas Nelson, 1990

Hill, S. *Fitness Challenge Activity Ideas* Booklet. A resource for playleaders. The University of Hull, 1993

The Health Promoting Playground. Available from: Health Promotion Wales, Ffynnon-las, Ty Glas Avenue, Llanishen, Cardiff CF4 5DZ

GAMES AND ATHLETIC ACTIVITIES

Cooper, A. *The Development of Games and Athletic Skills*. Simon and Schuster, 1993

Cooper, A. *Starting Games Skills*. Stanley Thornes, 1995

Devon County Council. *A Devon Approach to Teaching Games*. Devon Learning Resources, 1994

Devon County Council. *Athletic Activities*. Devon Learning Resources, 1996

DANCE

Evans, J. and Powell, H. *Inspirations for Dance and Movement*. Scholastic Publications, 1994

Harrison, K. *Look! Look! What I can do! Creative Dance Ideas for the Under Sevens*. BBC, 1992

Harrison, K. *Let's Dance: The Place of Dance in the Primary School*. Hodder and Stoughton

Harlow, M. and Rolfe, L. *Let's Dance*. BBC, 1992

Upton, E. and Paine, L. *Up the Sides and Down the Middle*. Southgate/Folk South West, 1996

Gibson, W. *Bruegel* (World of Art Series). Thames and Hudson, London, 1997

GYMNASTIC ACTIVITIES

Underwood, M. *Agile*, Nelson, 1991

Williams, A. *Curriculum Gymnastics*. Hodder and Stoughton, 1997

OUTDOOR AND ADVENTUROUS ACTIVITIES

Orienteering in the National Curriculum; A Practical Guide. Available from: Adventure Education, 12 St Andrew's Churchyard, Penrith CA11 7YE

The Guide Association. *Camps and Holidays*. The Guide Association, 1995

GENERAL

Chedzoy, S. *Physical Education for Teachers and Coordinators at Key Stages 1 and 2*. David Fulton, 1996

Wetton, P. *Physical Education in the Early Years*. Routledge, 1997

RESOURCE PACKS

Teaching Physical Education at Key Stages 1 and 2. (Guidelines and lesson plans for all Programmes of Study). Physical Education Association of the United Kingdom, 1995

The Dance Pack: *Dancing Across the Primary Curriculum.* Devon County Council. Torquay: Devon Resources, 1996

At the Heart of Education – Exercise and Heart Health. British Heart Foundation. London.

The Great Playtimes Games Kit. Available from: The National Playing FIelds Association, 25 Ovington Square, London. SW3 1LQ

Health Education Authority. *Happy Heart's Playground Games Pack.* Thomas Nelson & Sons, 1994

Useful organisations

GENERAL

Physical Education Association of the United Kingdom (PEA UK)
Ling House
Building L 25
London Road
Reading
RG1 5AQ
Tel: 0118 931 6240
The Physical Education Association produces an excellent professional journal for Physical Education in the Primary School. *Primary P.E. Focus.*

ATHLETIC ACTIVITIES

Five Star Award Scheme
Westways
Upper Tadmarton
Nr. Banbury
Oxon 0X15 5TB

IBM Ten Step Award
141–143 Drury Lane
London WC2B STD

Milk in Action
Education Department
National Dairy Council
5–7 John Princes Street
London W1M OA

DANCE

National Dance Teachers' Association
Treasurer NDTA
29 Larkspur Avenue
Chasetown
Walsall
Staffordshire WS7 8SR

National Resource Centre for Dance
University of Surrey
Guilford
Surrey GU2 5XH

GYMNASTIC ACTIVITIES

Amateur Gymnastics Association
Ford Hall
Lilleshall NSC
Newport TF10 9NB

GAMES

National Cricket Association
Lord's Ground
London NW8 8QZ

The Football Association
9 Wyllyotts Place
Potters Bar
Hertfordshire EN6 2JH

All England Netball Association
Netball House
9 Paynes Park
Hitchin
Hertfordshire SG5 1EH

Rugby Football Union
Resource Centre
Nortonthorp Mills
Scissett
Huddersfield
HD8 9LA

National Rounders Association
3 Denehurst Avenue
Nottingham NG8 5DA

National Badminton Centre
Bradwell Road
Loughton Lodge
Milton Keynes MK8 9LA

English Mini-Basketball Association
44 Northleat Avenue
Paignton
Devon TQ3 3UG

The Lawn Tennis Association Trust
The Queens Club
West Kensington
London W14 9EG

The English Volleyball Association
27 South Road
West Bridgford
Nottingham NG2 7AG

The Hockey Association
6 St John's
Worcester WR2 5AH

Pop Lacrosse
All England Women's Lacrosse Association
4 Western Court
Bromley Street
Digbeth
Birmingham B9 4AN

** Magic Mac Awards
for details write BP Thistle Awards
Caledonian House
South Gyle
Edinburgh EH2 9DQ

HEALTH EDUCATION

The Health Education Authority
Hamilton House
Mabledon Place
London
WC1H 9TX

OUTDOOR AND ADVENTUROUS ACTIVITIES

Advisory Association for Rope Courses and Initiatives (AARCI)

Mr Mike Forth
Salford Youth Centre
108 Ringlow Park Road
Swinton
Lancs M27 OHD

British Orienteering Federation
Riversdale
Dale Road North
Darley Dale
Matlock
Derbyshire DE4 2JB

The Guide Association
17-19 Buckingham Palace Road
London SW1W 0PT

The Scout Association
Baden Powell House
Queen's Gate
London SW7 5JS

National Association for Outdoor Education
305 The Argent Centre
60 Fredrick Street
Birmingham B1 3HS

Rope Course Developments Ltd
Burnbake
Rempstone
Corfe Castle
Wareham
Dorset BH20 5JH